MW00423444

Praise for Daddy Caddy on the Bag

Daddy Caddy on the Bag is just the right book, at just the right time. Our mission is to help kids have fun learning the life-long game of golf and to encourage family interaction that builds lasting memories. *Daddy Caddy on the Bag* goes right to the heart of this mission with its emphasis on fun and parent-child relationships. More than a golf instruction book, *Daddy Caddy on the Bag* will help you work cooperatively with your child as a coach and teammate, with the goal of developing your child into a golfer for life. A 'must read' for every golfing parent, *Daddy Caddy on the Bag* is the perfect complement to our junior golf products and tournament offerings.

Dan Van Horn, Founder and President, U.S. Kids Golf, Inc.

This book gave me the insight on how to let my boys grow and develop at their own pace, without any pushing. *Daddy Caddy on the Bag* has helped me not only to be a better teammate with my kids on the golf course, but to have a better relationship overall with them, on and off the golf course.

Carlos Baez

Daddy Caddy on the Bag is a must read to anyone getting their child and themselves into the greatest sport, golf. The book also has so many parallels to all the other youth sports. Thank you Rick for the insight you have given me to help be a positive influence on my sons. Since reading *Daddy Caddy on the Bag*, my son has really blossomed!!

Mike Wylie

Thanks to the many good suggestions in *Daddy Caddy on the Bag*, we won a national tournament in Mexico and my son is now number one in this country. The training part of the book helped us to achieve this goal. Thank you Rick!

Pablo Barbachano

Congratulations, you wrote a wonderful book, which should be given to most parents at any golf federation. I will try to adopt your advice. I thought that I was doing a good job with my son, but your book showed me that there is still much room for me to improve as a Daddy Caddy!

José Luis Alvarez de Soto

My boys enjoyed playing the practice round with you and Alex at Jekyll Island. I just finished your book and think it is a must read for any child wanting to play golf or any parent wanting their child to play golf, especially tournament golf. It is a tough act balancing the different "roles" we parents play in the lives of our children and I think you offered some valuable insight to how to separate those roles and duties.

Ben Bowen

Love your book! Have read it twice! I recommend it to the parents of all my students, as well as all the families I meet while running Hampton Roads U.S Kids Golf Tour. Would go as far as to say it's probably the best golf book I have ever read ...Millions of juniors will meet their true potential in golf because of this book.

Michelle Holmes, Director, Michelle Holmes School of Golf

Other books by Rick Heard

Daddy Caddy Off the Bag: Tournament Time!

The ParKit Golf Encyclopedia of Fun Golf Games

The ParKit Golf Skills Improvement Workbook

The ParKit Golf Book of Fun Golf Games for Kids

Daddy Caddy
On the Bag

*Coach Your Child
To Peak Golf Performance*

Second Edition

Rick Heard, PGA

ARD PRESS

Published by ARD Publishing
Boca Raton, Florida

Printed in the United States of America

Text and cover design by Rick Heard

Cover photograph by Tim Barbini

Spanish translation by Jose Luis Alvarez de Soto and Ines Ramos

 Like Daddy Caddy on the Bag on facebook

ISBN: 0-9786717-9-1
ISBN-13: 978-0-9786717-9-2

To **Mom** and **Dad**, *who gave me golf,*
to my wife **Diane**, *who gave me Alex,*
- and -
to **Alex**, *who gave me coaching lessons.*

CONTENTS

ACKNOWLEDGMENTS

I am grateful to all of those who steered me toward a mid-life career change that led to becoming a PGA member and teaching professional. That change led me to my wonderful wife Diane, which in turn produced our amazing son Alex. I thank them for their patience with all of my projects. Their support, understanding and love made this book possible.

I could not have joined the PGA if it were not for Don and Diana Law, who gave me the opportunity to explore my passion for teaching golf. Don's love for junior golf is unbounded, and his creativity and energy and focus on keeping it fun have made him nationally known as "Mr. Junior Golf." Don and Diana have been great friends and business partners through the Don Law Golf Academy and ParKit Golf. Somewhere along the line I think it was Diana who one day said to me "you should write a book."

The idea for this book came to me from first-hand experiences caddying for Alex in junior tournaments and observing the moms and dads and kids trying to sort through so many conflicting roles. I am thankful to all of these "daddy caddies" and golfers who have shown me the complete spectrum of relationships, from unimaginably bad to wonderfully good.

Because of those tournaments, I am grateful for our U.S. Kids local tour staff, led by Jennifer Moss. Jennifer runs six local U.S. Kids tours, encompassing some 34 tournaments annually. My son wants to compete in all of them.

I am also thankful for Lisa deMartino, who coordinates our junior classes and camp programs at the Don Law Golf Academy. The wonderful kids who attend our classes have taught me how to relate to junior golfers and how to make our programs fun, interesting, and educational. Lisa somehow manages to keep all of them, and their parents, happy and coming back for more.

I appreciate the feedback and suggestions from Margo Cohen, Team Baez, Team Wylie, and Team Smith who graciously gave me some of their time in reviewing draft versions. Their encouragement and feedback were invaluable and helped shape the scope of this book. Carson, Cameron, Bryce, Tyler, JT, and Andie are the future of golf.

My parents gave the gift of golf to me when I was only five or six years old, and they allowed me to grow up on and around the DeLand Country Club. I am eternally grateful to them for their patience and understanding when I would return home from the golf course to a meal that was no longer warm, full of stories about birdies, pars, and bogies. Sadly, the club where I played more than 1,000 rounds of golf as a boy closed in late 2012.

One of the great things about golf is the wonderful people you meet in and around the golf course. We were fortunate to meet Daddy Caddy José Luis Alvarez and his amazing son Diego at a regional U.S. Kids tournament near Tampa. We became friends and José volunteered to translate the book into Spanish. I owe a million thanks to José and his lovely wife Patricia for their efforts in creating the Spanish version of "Daddy Caddy on the Bag."

Finally, I am thankful for Alex, who is an incredible boy and an outstanding golfer. He has shown me how to be a dad, coach, mentor and caddy. Although he has "fired" and "rehired" me a few times, I'm still on the bag and intend to stay there. I only hope that I can heed my own advice and be the best golf coach he could ever have.

FOREWORD

I think that given a choice when embarking for an unfamiliar destination, we would all prefer to have a road map. The world of competitive junior golf is just such a journey, mostly without any "maps."

My relationship with Rick and Alex has given me a microscopic view of their education in golf. I have witnessed the growth of Alex as a player and Rick as his coach and caddy (and daddy!). More importantly, I have watched their evolution as a team. I have seen that the frustrations of golf are undeniably absorbed better with a partner at your side.

This book is about far more than golf... it is also about the bond between a parent and a child. Rick's insight to golf is educational but his story of devotion to Alex is INSPIRATIONAL.

No matter the obstacle or the journey, a large dose of love and compassion will overcome the small details like a missed putt.

Here is your road map. Enjoy your journey.

Don Law, PGA
October, 2012

INTRODUCTION

I first wrote this book because caddying for my then seven-year old son Alex in competitive golf tournaments was the most challenging, stress-inducing, anger-generating, exasperating, exciting, fulfilling, and satisfying job I had ever had. And I am a PGA golf professional who has been around golf for 50 years! So, as I help Alex and watch the other parent-child teams on the junior golf tours, I know that the job of the "daddy caddy" probably isn't any easier for them.

It is now two years later, and Alex is nearly 10. A lot has happened in those two short years, and it is time for a few enhancements to this book.

Over these two years since "Daddy Caddy on the Bag" came to life, we have played in some 80 junior golf tournaments, including local U.S. Kids tours, ten U.S. Kids regional events (two of which he won), the U.S. Kids European Championships, the U.S. Kids World Championships (twice), the Callaway Junior World Championships, the Junior Honda Classic, and the Doral-Publix Junior Golf Classic (which he won).

The concepts and philosophies behind "Daddy Caddy on the Bag" have been well-received, and I have had the opportunity to conduct parent-child seminars both in the USA and oversees to more than 300 people. My interactions with seminar attendees and discussions with many parents, and feedback on the book have shown a hunger for more information and more depth on a few of the main topics.

I have addressed some of these with "Daddy Caddy Off the Bag," a book for kids that tackles many of the issues they face in becoming responsible, independent young men and women and golfers. However, I am convinced that more can be offered to parents, for whom "Daddy Caddy on the Bag" is written.

That new material is here; much of it in chapter three on the mental game, but also throughout the book with a new section in chapter five on early specialization and elsewhere with updates and more detail and advice.

We all struggle with the same challenges. We want our children to succeed and to make us proud. We want them to overcome gracefully the adversity that comes their way on and off the course. Most of all, we want them to become golfers for life; to truly love this great game. We know that the lessons and values taught by the game of golf will be invaluable to them as they grow to adulthood. And, we know that their ability to play golf will be one of the greatest assets they can have for the rest of their lives.

However, becoming a golfer is a long term process; and it doesn't matter how well one plays at 6 years old, or even at 10 years old. What matters is that our children remain interested, continue to see golf as fun, and still love the game when they are in their teens… when their foundation in golf can combine with inspiration and really take them somewhere.

So, this book was written in part to help me come to terms with the task of being my son's coach and caddy, and in part to help others who may not have the depth of background in golf that I am fortunate to have.

Who Are You?

You are a parent with a child who is interested in golf. Or, perhaps you *want* your child to be interested in golf. Or, you may be well past the introductory stages and your child is already a golfer or even a competitive tournament player. Regardless, your mission is to help your child reach his or her potential in golf. It isn't an easy task. Golf is perhaps the most difficult and demanding game ever invented, and beginners and experts alike are continually challenged by its mental and physical requirements. Being a parent is demanding itself, and when parenting combines with coaching and caddying for your child – well now you have a real challenge.

These are formative years for your child, when coordination, talent, and interest can be nurtured and developed into a lifelong love of what I firmly believe is the world's greatest game. Whether or not your child possesses the necessary skills to compete at high levels is largely irrelevant, because the value of golf is much greater than winning tournaments.

Golf teaches respect, integrity, honor, patience, responsibility, perseverance, honesty, humility, and virtually every core value that is important throughout our lives. It can be extremely satisfying and frustrating at the same time. You can provide the opportunity for your child to experience golf, but fair warning: before you know it you may find yourself falling deeper and deeper into the game. Naturally, your child will look to you for swing advice as though you were his PGA/LPGA teaching professional.

In no time at all you will probably be juggling the conflicting roles of being your child's golf coach, mentor, and caddy... on top of being his or her parent. For young children just learning golf, this is a normal situation that I see all of the time, and it can be a great experience. It can also be extremely frustrating for all involved, and if not handled properly by you, it can leave a lasting negative impression on your child that can drive him or her away from the game.

So this book is addressed to you, the parent who wants to navigate the fairways of golf with your young child. By "young," I mean from age 2-12, give or take a year. Once your child reaches around age 11-12, he or she will be less reliant on you as a coach and caddy. And, by then his or her interest in playing competitive golf can skyrocket, and serious performance training can occur. If it doesn't... no problem. He or she will still have a foundation in golf that will serve them later in their business or professional careers.

But, how do you bring your child to that stage? How do you start your toddler in golf? How do you coach and develop and bring out his or her best performance on the golf course? How do you remain friends with your child in spite of golf?

Who Am I?

I am a golfer. Like many, I was introduced to the game at an early age by my dad. Although no pro, he was a good player who occasionally shot in the 70's once a week with his friends on Saturday mornings. I don't remember getting hooked on golf, but it happened with cut-down, steel-shafted, heavy as lead muscle-back irons and persimmon headed woods from the 1960's... then later on with my mom's Patty Berg clubs.

Playing opportunities were limited, formal instruction was almost non-existent, and junior tournaments were scarce, but I found golfing friends, fed off the internal challenge of the game and became a very good player. My friends and I virtually grew up on the golf course, and played as much golf as we could. I won the Florida State Junior PGA Championships along with a few other junior tournaments, led my high school team to three championship seasons, and was a member of the University of Florida golf team.

I always thought I would be a golf pro, but one thing led to another and after graduating from UF, I took a research job in Boston and got away from golf for a few years. In reality, I was a bit burned out from years of practice and playing, and the combination of an exciting job and a break from golf was very enticing.

I played socially for a few years, but I missed competitive golf. When a job change led me back to Florida, I dived in again and tuned up my game, winning two city championships, three county championships, and finishing 5th in the Florida State Amateur. After 22 years in the corporate world, the siren call of golf was too strong, and I left my job to pursue my passions of playing and teaching golf.

To become a PGA professional, I had to pass a playing ability test, which consists of a one-day, 36 hole competition. In order to pass, I had to score within 15 strokes of the course rating for the two rounds. In my case, the target score was 155, equal to rounds of 77-78. It was intimidating to know beforehand what I had to shoot, but I treated it like an ordinary tournament, shot 68-73, and was medalist. Of 110 golfers in the field, only around 10 made the cut.

Once you pass the PAT, you attend PGA school, which consists of a combination of self-study and seminars where you learn all about the business of golf. There are three levels, and each level generally takes one year to complete. I completed all three in six months, winning the Acushnet scholarship for the highest score on each level. During all of this, I began working with my friend and fellow PGA professional Don Law, where we built a strong reputation teaching and mentoring junior golfers. I say "we" because I was there, but Don gets all of the credit. He is the consummate PGA professional and leader, and he created one of the largest and best junior golf programs in the world. He was recognized as the national PGA Junior Leader in 2012, the most prestigious junior golf award in the country. It was richly deserved.

During my first 10 years as a PGA professional, I was recognized in the Southeast Chapter of the South Florida PGA as Junior Leader (2002), and won the PGA Horton Smith education award twice (2007 and 2008). I also won the Southeast Chapter PGA Golf Professional of the Year award in 2010, and was president of the Southeast Chapter PGA for three terms (6 years, ending in 2012). I ran the tournament committee and served as a PGA rules official in junior events. I also led the creation of ParKit Golf, Inc., a company founded by Don Law, his wife Diana, Bill Scott, Chad Kurmel, and me to help other teaching pros enhance their own junior golf programs.

I mention all of this because I have been there. I've been a junior golfer, played middle school and high school golf, made it on the University of Florida college golf team, played in perhaps 100 amateur tournaments, turned pro, played in dozens of PGA club pro events, taught more than 5,000 lessons, and I co-own and manage the Don Law Golf Academy in Boca Raton. Through our academy's various programs, we encompass upwards of 1,000 junior golfers from age 4 to 18.

Now, as a dad and caddy, I have come full-circle. I have been "on the bag" for nearly 200 rounds of tournament golf as Alex's caddy, and I have seen it all. I know how it feels to take the blame for every poor shot hit by my son ("wrong club, Dad"). I know how it feels to watch a train wreck happen on the fourth hole ("why didn't you aim me"?). I regularly press my foot against an imaginary brake when one of his putts goes zooming past the hole. I've seen dads and moms screaming at their young golfers. I've heard the sarcastic remarks from parents that leave their child feeling empty ("I guess you like making bogies!"). I've heard a young golfer say that his dad would be mad at him for hitting that drive into the rough. I've spoken with dozens of parents wanting to know how they can better support and encourage their children in golf. And, I've experienced the incredible satisfaction of simply playing golf with my son.

About This Book

This book will help you bring out the best in your child on the golf course. After all, isn't that what all of us parents / caddies really want? But sometimes it seems that golf can bring out the worst in us – and the worst in our children. Oh, how easy it is for us to forget how difficult golf can be! How hard it is to make a 3-foot putt; how challenging it is to curb your ego and hit the smart layup shot; how tough it is to lag a 50 footer up next to the hole; and how much trouble bunker shots can be. Make no mistake. Playing golf is difficult. So is caddying!

Therefore, this book dives right in and begins with how to leave your parenting hat in the car and be the best caddy you can be. But there is so much more to the challenge of the game and teaching golf to your child. Thus, this book also covers everything from starting your child in golf to describing a model player development program that you can use to help take your junior golfer to the highest levels of performance.

This book will help you become a better coach and caddy. It will also help you understand and appreciate your junior golfer and the challenges he or she faces. If golfers in general are a different breed – and we are – junior golfers are even more so. It is the rare child who can focus on something for 2 ½ hours. It is equally rare to find those who have the hand-eye coordination and physical skills necessary to hit a golf ball consistently.

It is rarer still for a child to be able to control their golf ball's distance, trajectory, and direction sufficient to play golf and keep score. It is a very special child who can put all of these skills together, play nine holes of golf under tournament conditions, follow USGA rules, and shoot scores in the 30's and 40's from age-appropriate tees. And, it is even more challenging for them to play 18 holes of tournament golf over a six-hour timeframe in hammering rain, cold, wind, or heat!

Yet, such is the world of the junior tournament golfer, and this world is filled with talented children and dedicated parents. It is for these children and their parents that I wrote this book.

Although I am a huge supporter of junior girl golfers, having taught dozens of them in private lessons, group classes, and camps, I decided to use masculine pronouns throughout this book. Therefore, I frequently refer to your junior golfer as "he" or "him," just for ease of reading. Please do not get the idea that this book is just for boys, or that any of my suggestions do not apply to girls. People are people, and golf is golf. The game and our parent-child relationships are gender-neutral. Where possible, I use both "him and her" or "he and she," and sometimes simply "player." And my use of "you" and "your" is directed at you, the parent(s) of your junior golfer, whether you are a "daddy caddy" or a "mom caddy."

What is a "Daddy Caddy"?

Nine principles define what I believe to be the essence of a "Daddy Caddy." These nine principles can serve to guide your actions and direction as you coach and develop your child's golf game.

Being a Daddy Caddy means adopting a certain philosophy and following proven principles of coaching and development as applied to golf. Many fathers (and mothers too) caddy for their children. Many struggle with balancing the parent/coach/caddy relationship – I know I do. This book defines how to make it work while maintaining your sanity and, as I say, remain friends with your child in spite of golf.

I initially was going to use that as the subtitle for this book. However, as I thought about it, I realized that not everyone *wants* to be friends with their children. At least, that is not so important to everyone. What we all do want is to bring out the best in our children, whether on the golf course or in any activity. The book focuses on that goal, so its subtitle is "Coach Your Child to Peak Golf Performance."

For me, friendship with my son is most important, and through that friendship, I believe I can help him be the best that he can be and reach his personal peak. The book doesn't require parents and children to be friends, but it does describe how to play the roles of parent, caddy, and coach for the benefit of your child.

My nine Daddy Caddy principles are these:

1. Keep it Fun
2. Think Long Term
3. Under-Coach
4. Make it Social
5. Teach Humility
6. Golf is (Not) Life
7. Show Patience
8. Be a Teammate
9. Play Golf

Daddy Caddy Principle #1

Keep it Fun

Golf should be fun. I don't mean that every moment on the practice range must be fun, and I know that not every moment on the course is fun. However, on balance, the game must be fun - both for us and for our kids. Why else would we do it? So, while you are out there, ask yourself periodically "am I having fun?" "Is my child enjoying himself or herself?" Think of times that were fun for all and how well things went, and how your child couldn't wait to go back to the golf course the next time. Think also of times that were not fun and how you got through them. Here is an example:

A the 2012 U.S. Kids Holiday Classic, my son was in a foul mood during the first round, and was upset at nearly everything. He was angry after making a fantastic par save from a greenside bunker on the third hole ("should have been on the green with a birdie putt, dad"). Although he was one-under par at the time, I'll confess that I threatened to take him off the course if he kept it up. We were not having fun.

I tried to put it into perspective for him – about the importance of a par and being thankful for making the most of a bad situation. And, about not appearing arrogant in front his fellow competitors who were not scoring as well. Somehow, he hung in there and finished the round even par. After the round we discussed it at length and I emphasized the importance of his attitude. Isn't golf about 99.9% mental, at least once the mechanics are there?

The next day he acted like the best model golfer I have ever seen, handling things like a tour pro and never getting rattled, even after starting with a bogey. His game reflected his attitude, and he shot 2-under par and won his age group. It was great fun. Was there a connection?

Unfortunately, most examples of this principle are those where kids and parents are definitely not having fun. One I personally witnessed was a boy whose father pinched him during a practice round at the World Championships. I saw nothing wrong other than that the boy wasn't playing his best. Was he having any fun? Why would he want to come back to the golf course?

Bruce E. Brown and Rob Miller of Proactive Coaching LLC are former coaches turned youth athlete advocates, and their study of elite college athletes is eye-opening. They surveyed hundreds of college athletes, who were asked about their worst memory from playing youth and high school sports. Their overwhelming response was "the ride home from games with my parents."

We have all experienced that ride, either as the driver or as the unfortunate occupant strapped into the back seat. That ride is not fun, and it can ruin the entire golf experience and make your child want to stop playing golf.

My challenge to you is this: make the ride home the same regardless of your experience on the course. If you were going to stop for ice cream but had a bad day – whether from the caddy-player relationship or from simply playing poorly – then stop for ice cream anyway. If there is something that needs to be discussed, sleep on it and talk about it the next day when emotions have cooled.

So, the concept of "keep it fun" applies everywhere: on the practice range, on the course in informal play, in tournaments, and in the aftermath, on the ride home and afterward.

Daddy Caddy Principle #2

Think Long Term

Golf is a marathon – not a sprint. Marathon runners pace themselves and are prepared for the long haul. Golf is the same – especially junior golf. I can't put into words how difficult it is to watch by the sidelines and observe the slow, steady progress my son makes. It is excruciatingly painful. And, I can't express how hard it is to keep a long-term perspective, especially when I want him to do well now. But the truth is that nothing that happens now, when he is so young, really matters!

I know that his experiences now will be valuable, and all of his tournament play will provide a solid foundation for the future. But it is that future that really matters, and as a Daddy Caddy, I can only take actions now that help ensure that his future includes golf.

So, the second principle of being a Daddy Caddy is to take a long-term perspective and keep a focus on the future. Keep your child interested now, while he or she is young, by keeping it fun (Daddy Caddy Principle #1), and aim to have your child love golf as a teenager and beyond.

It is fantastic if he or she plays well now. It is great to win at a young age and build confidence. However, I can think of so many instances where a young superstar won everything, only to burn out early and watch kids who started golf at a later age push them aside. I want my child to have that fire and motivation when he is a teenager. I wish he had it now, but he is too young to understand and to focus on only one sport.

So hear this Daddy Caddies: think long term. Enjoy the early successes, but don't sweat the tough times. Keep it fun, and pace yourselves. Golf is forever.

Daddy Caddy Principle #3

Under-Coach

The less you coach, the more they learn. A Daddy Caddy doesn't over coach.

When I think of coaching my son, my first thoughts go back to teaching him to ride a bicycle. Like most, he began with training wheels. Then, I devised a "control stick" made of a 5-iron stuck between the rear fork of the bike frame. Funny that I used a golf club for this task!

Training wheels off, I used the club to help him balance while running alongside him on the bike. Whenever he felt balanced, I let go of the club, but I kept running along, ready to grab the club if he lost control. Many times, he didn't even know I had let go, so he wasn't worried about balancing… he just kept pedaling. Soon, the club wasn't needed and he was riding on his own, full of new confidence and the self-satisfaction of accomplishing a major new objective on his own, or so he thought.

Shouldn't golf be that way?

What I mean is this. When we think about it, our kids are going to be playing golf by themselves very soon. Your kids may already be playing on their own. If the goal is to get them there, then why not begin the process now? Grab the control stick only when really needed to prevent disaster. However, usually there is too much "coaching" going on before every shot.

Most of it is us trying to control every move our child makes. "Aim a little more left. More. A little more. Oops… too much… back to the right. OK. Now, focus on your target. Get your ball a little more on your left side. Now aim a bit more to the left. No. The other left. OK. Look at your target. Now, keep your head steady, take a smooth backswing, and swing out fast. OK. GO!"

If this sounds anything like what you do, take a step back and think about how hard it would be for you to hit a good shot if I was directing you like that. Sooner or later, our kids need to break free and do their own thing. Start by letting them play each shot by themselves in practice. Then, try it in a tournament. You may be surprised how well they do, and best of all, they will "own" their result. That's right... whatever happens won't be your fault, dad. Remember Daddy Caddy principle #2: think long term? It won't matter if they hit a bad shot now, and if you aren't playing puppeteer, so much the better. Plus, if everything does fall apart, you can always step back in and grab that control stick if needed.

Yes, it is hard to let go, and deep down we all want our child to need us. I want my son to need me too, but I'm a much better coach when I can let go of that control stick and let him solo, with a little guidance as needed. I don't want him to get hurt, but its okay for him to make some mistakes and learn from them. And when he does, he is again filled with the joy of accomplishing something on his own.

Daddy Caddy Principle #4

Make it Social

Four years ago, I wasn't really sure my son was enjoying golf. He split time between tennis and golf camps, and tennis went to the top of his list of "favorites." Don't get me wrong, I love tennis, and I always played both tennis and golf. And I am not in favor of concentrating on just one sport at an early age. Diversity, as always, is good. But, I confess I was just a bit concerned that golf wasn't doing it for him.

Although we played and practiced golf together whenever possible, I'm sure from his perspective it just wasn't that much fun hanging out with old dad all of the time (it hurts when I say that!). Then it happened. He found some new friends and a couple of older kids he admired at golf camp and golf rocketed back to the top of his list. I was delighted that he wanted to be at the golf course. He still plays tennis, but golf is number one.

Suddenly, golf was fun (Daddy Caddy principle #1) and he couldn't wait to get to the course each day for golf camp with his buddies. There is nothing better than getting a group of junior golfers together and letting them feed off one another. So much learning goes on as the younger ones try to emulate the older and better players, and the competitive juices flow with each challenge. It is a social thing, and it makes perfect sense. I love teaching golf camps, and we create a fun social environment with teams and competitive games that bring the kids together. Other kids provide role models and the group setting makes for endless fun games and challenges for everyone.

A Daddy Caddy seeks out the social environment and allows his or her child to flourish in the company of golf buddies. That is how I grew up, and I don't know of any successful pro who lived a solitary life of golf with no camaraderie or social network. It may take some effort, because golf is a solitary sport and we golfers are independent, sometimes to a fault. But the rewards are worth the effort.

It is amazing to watch what happens when kids go out on the course together and play a few holes on their own, without us hovering over them. You will quickly find out that your child is capable of getting around the golf course without your Daddy Caddy help. You will still be needed at tournament time, but the experience of playing golf with friends will make your child a better player by thinking, making decisions, and accepting the consequences of his or her actions.

And, beyond all of the fog of caddying and coaching your junior golfer, remember that the long-term goal is to create a golfer. Great things happen socially with golf – whether with friends or negotiating a business deal. Show your child that social environment and watch him or her become a golfer for life.

Daddy Caddy Principle #5

Teach Humility

Humility is an interesting word because it is often misunderstood as being meek or timid. I prefer Wikipedia's definition: "the quality of being modest and respectful." In the language of golf, humility means "let your clubs do the talking," and in fact it may be one of the greatest lessons that golf can teach.

It turns out that humility is one of the key characteristics of great leaders, and it is the antithesis of arrogance and conceit. Any search about humility will quickly point to Level 5 leadership, which is based on the idea that great leaders exhibit respect toward others, selflessness, and a strong commitment to achieving results. Humility is having a quiet confidence without the need for overselling ourselves. It's about being content to let others discover the layers of our talents without having to boast about them. It's a lack of arrogance, not a lack of aggressiveness in the pursuit of achievement.

As it does in so many other ways, golf mirrors life, and it rewards humility.

Just listen to any PGA or LPGA Tour pro winner's acceptance speech. They speak of their good fortune, of the skills of their competitors, of the quality of the golf course, and of the sponsors' generosity. They don't gloat in victory and magnify their personal accomplishments. They are modest and respectful, and in so doing, they win our support and we become their fans.

Humility also has religious roots, but I'll focus my thoughts on what we all know as "the golf gods." I can say with great authority and from years of experience that any time I thought I had figured the game out, perfected my swing, got cocky or greedy, or otherwise thought arrogant thoughts about how well I was playing, the golf gods quickly showed me otherwise. And therein lies our Daddy Caddy duty to teach our children humility.

I love this parable, and I think it is relevant, so here goes:

> An old Cherokee told his grandson, "My son, there is a battle between two wolves inside us all. One is Evil. It is anger, jealousy, greed, resentment, inferiority, lies and ego. The other is Good. It is joy, peace, love, hope, humility, kindness, empathy, and truth." The boy thought about it, and asked, "Grandfather, which wolf wins?" The old man quietly replied, "The one you feed."

As Daddy Caddies, we need to help our young golfers learn to feed the right wolf. It has to do with respecting themselves, the golf course and the game. About etiquette and honesty. About respecting other golfers and recognizing their abilities. About recognizing their own weaknesses and resolving to improve. About suffering the punishment that golf is sure to deliver on a regular basis and still persevering. About being gracious in both victory and defeat. About maintaining an even keel through the highs and lows of a single round of golf. And, ultimately, about letting their clubs do the talking.

These are all traits we want our kids to have, and golf will teach them with your Daddy Caddy help.

Daddy Caddy Principle #6

Golf is (Not) Life

We have all heard the metaphor "golf is life." In so many ways, it is. The values important in golf – things like honesty, respect, integrity, perseverance, courtesy, and responsibility – are those of life. Golf and life both change constantly with our internal beings and with external factors. Both supply us with highs and lows by the hour, or even by the minute. Both require us to look inward and discover ourselves, our ambitions, our capabilities, and to face our fears. Both allow us to succeed and test us in failure. Yes, golf is much like life.

Thankfully, it isn't.

Remembering that fact is Daddy Caddy Principle #6. The importance of this understanding is clear when we think of our own self worth or our opinions or statements to our golfing children. A bad shot does not make one a bad person. It is only a bad shot. A poor score is not indicative of a person's intelligence or value. Golf is surely difficult, and it will test us to our core. But, in the end, it is only golf.

As Daddy Caddies, we need to keep this in mind as we

judge our children and others on the golf course. Just as hitting a great shot does not make your child a good person, hitting a poor shot does not mean that he or she is bad. Again, it is only a bad shot. It wasn't intentional. Golf and life both throw curveballs at us. What matters is how we recover and move on. A Daddy Caddy helps his or her child understand and cope with these challenges, dealing with setbacks and remaining focused on the bigger picture.

No, golf is not life. It just feels like it.

Daddy Caddy Principle #7

Show Patience

Golf teaches us nothing if not patience. We wait for an open station on the range. We wait for the first tee to be open. We wait for the green to clear. We wait for our young golfer to mature (and, once there, we long for the good old days). We wait for them to learn the value of a single golf stroke.

Patience may be one of the most difficult Daddy Caddy principles to achieve. I love Wikipedia's definition:

Patience (from Wikipedia):

Patience is the state of endurance under difficult circumstances, which can mean persevering in the face of delay or provocation without acting on annoyance/anger in a negative way; or exhibiting forbearance when under strain, especially when faced with longer-term difficulties. Patience is the level of endurance one can take before negativity.

Coaching your child certainly produces "difficult circumstances" and "provocation", leading to "annoyance/anger" requiring "endurance!"

Oddly enough, we can be patient about some things and impatient about others. I think our level of patience is based on our expectations. We can be quite patient waiting in a long line to vote, or waiting to buy something on sale on "black Friday." We know it will take a long time, so we wait without complaint. But, we will honk at the car in front if it doesn't start moving the moment the traffic light changes.

It is the same when it comes to your child playing golf. In a big way, patience for us means not giving up too soon on a practice session, a round of golf, or a swing change. The challenge for us Daddy Caddies is remembering Daddy Caddy Principle #2 and thinking long term. Expect golf to be difficult. Expect there to be struggles. Expect failures – and successes.

If we are truly thinking long term, we can wait patiently for skills to develop and scores to reflect those skills. If we expect miracles, we will be disappointed and become impatient. Daddy Caddy patience is about enduring those difficult circumstances that face us every time we hit the links. Your child just wants to play on the practice green, without doing those drills? Be patient – there is still some learning going on. He or she starts the round poorly? Be patient – there is still a lot of golf to play.

It can be incredibly difficult to remain patient while your child is struggling on the course, but as a Daddy Caddy, this could be a time that valuable lessons are being learned. I have seen big leads evaporate late in the round in favor of the golfer who remained patient and kept plugging along. I have seen a horrible start turn into a great round due to positive thinking and not giving up. These things may or may not happen, but you can be sure they won't if you give up too soon.

Daddy Caddy Principle #8

Be a Teammate

When many of us play golf, it is in a team environment such as a charity scramble, a corporate league, or a four-ball at the club. However, tournament golf can be a lonely, solitary sport that challenges our very being. Even in those team-oriented golf events, we look to ourselves for blame, and it can be quite difficult to live up to our own expectations. Most other sports allow us a scapegoat, since losses can be blamed on teammates or opponents.

When we play golf, everything that happens is our own fault. It is us against the course; us against nature; and us against ourselves.

Accepting that challenge takes courage, maturity, and responsibility, and that is a lot to ask of a young golfer. As his or her Daddy Caddy, your child needs a teammate. When you listen to PGA or LPGA tour pros discuss their round, you will hear them say things like "we hit an 8-iron" or "we misjudged the wind." The operative word is "we", and as my mom used to say, that is a little word with a big meaning.

Being a teammate means making decisions together as partners, working for a common cause. In this case, that cause is your child's long-term love of the game. In some ways, it is the most difficult Daddy Caddy principle to follow, because it means we must accept blame for the errors of our children. However, that is part of the caddy's job, and it is also a key part of your role as a coach.

Even though your child is ultimately responsible for everything that happens to his or her golf ball and your role as a caddy and coach is more akin to that of an advisor, remember that everyone needs a little support now and then. And, remember that challenges such as those provided by golf are easier for your child to face when shared with a loving teammate and partner – his or her Daddy Caddy.

Daddy Caddy Principle #9

Play Golf

While Daddy Caddy Principles 1 - 8 are largely philosophical, number nine is practical. Play golf. With your child. Together.

We spend so much time coaching our children on the range and caddying and coaching them on the golf course. Maybe it is different for you, but sometimes I just need to get away from that and simply enjoy playing golf with my son.

I try (I really do) just to let him be my partner, or maybe my opponent, on the course. It isn't easy, but that is perhaps the ultimate reward for this journey. Nothing can rival the personal satisfaction of simply playing golf with your child.

There are so many reasons for this. It lets him see me being human and hitting poor shots and making mistakes – the same ones that I might criticize him for. It lets me see him making his own decisions and just enjoying the game. It lets us bond and enjoy a few hours together. It lets me model good etiquette and behavior in the face of challenges. And, it lets me see a little more of who he really is and who he may become without me hovering over him.

I think golf can provide the greatest connection between parent and child of any sport, but you have to get out there and do it together. Play golf.

· · ·

It isn't easy to abide by all of these principles, but they provide a guiding path to follow as our children's games develop. Many people are daddies, caddies, and coaches. Not everyone is a Daddy Caddy. I try every day to live up to these principles and to be one. I hope everyone can become a better Daddy Caddy by following these nine principles, and I believe that in so doing, we will be helping to grow the game of golf and to raise a new generation of respectful, responsible golfers.

Daddy Caddy
On the Bag

---

*Coach Your Child
To Peak Golf Performance*

CHAPTER ONE

"Wear one hat at a time."

Daddy Caddy on the Bag

It was a typical summer weekend afternoon in South Florida. Ominous storm clouds on the horizon threatened our planned practice round in spite of what the handheld weather app said. I pulled up to the bag drop and the attendant got to the trunk before me, loading my bag on the golf cart. "Not that one," I said. "Take this one," and I handed Alex's bag to the attendant. "I'm not playing today. Just caddying." I tossed my clubs back into the car to stares as Alex, all of four feet tall came over for help tying his shoes.

"*He's* playing?" the other attendant asked incredulously. I'm sure they did not understand how a five year old boy who couldn't tie his shoes could play golf. "Oh, he can play," I assured them, and we headed for the golf shop.

And so go our lives as daddy caddies, coaches, trainers, mentors, and teachers to our golfing sons and daughters. We sacrifice our own golf games and play vicariously through the clubs of our children. We try to teach them the game that we love but which we ourselves don't truly understand. We try to help our children manage their emotions when the golf gods get them the way they get us, even though we struggle to manage our own emotions. And we try to guide them in making wise stroke-saving decisions, when we ourselves would take the riskier shot.

Like you, I seek my way in the dark, hoping to give my child the best chance to grow into a golfer for life. Like you, I wonder whether he will be a serious player, earn a college scholarship, and perhaps become a tour pro someday. Perhaps unlike you, I know how difficult that road is, how unlikely it is that he will make it that far, and how little it matters right now. Although he says he wants to be a pro, that isn't something that I can imagine at this time. Frankly, I'm not even sure I would want him to lead that life.

But for now, we are daddy caddies on the bag, taking on the difficult challenge of wearing multiple hats and dealing with many of the same issues faced by all sports parents.

We see it all of the time on baseball and soccer fields. Parents shouting directions from the sidelines, admonishing their own kids for making mistakes while simultaneously consoling other parents whose kids do the same.

Golf parenting is much more difficult because there is no fence separating us from our child. We are there next to him, in the thick of things, succeeding and failing together, congratulating and blaming each other, and trying to sort out the differing roles we are playing. But how did we get to this point?

Most of us began innocently enough by bringing our kid(s) to the golf driving range and helping them attack a pile of range balls. We showed them how to hold the club, how to stand, and they watched us swing. Once he or she got the hang of things the plot thickened. How can we best help our child enjoy golf, succeed in hitting the ball, and grow into a golfer? For reasons of convenience, money, and the pure joy of experiencing the process with them, we frequently ease into the roles of being their golf coach, teacher, trainer, and mentor. And when they are ready to play on the course, we become their caddy. It is a slippery slope!

A tour professional may have several different people playing these roles, each specialists in their own field and working together for a common cause. Under the best of circumstances, these specialists focus on only their own areas of specialization and don't cross boundaries. For example, Ricky Fowler's caddy is not also his swing coach, and his swing coach is not his personal trainer. Our children have only us, and we know no boundaries! We caddy, coach, teach, train, and parent all at the same time, with predictable results.

If we are to succeed in coaching our children to peak golf performance, we need to specialize (or hire specialists) and stay within the boundaries of the role we are playing, when we are playing it. In other words, we need to wear one hat at a time.

For most of us, the thought of hiring specialists is akin to admitting failure. We can and want to do it ourselves, but we need some guidance. Moreover, nothing can equal the satisfaction we get as we bond with our son or daughter through golf. It isn't easy, but I wouldn't trade the experience for anything.

So, let's get down to business and clarify the roles and responsibilities of all of the people involved in our child's golf journey. I have chosen to begin with the end, so to speak, meaning we will begin with your job as caddy.

DADDY CADDY ON THE BAG

Who Does What?

In addition to our own multiple personalities, there are many other people involved in the world of junior golf. However, when it is tournament time, there are only a few different roles that matter. Aside from the junior golfer, or player, there are parents, spectators, coaches, trainers, teaching professionals, and caddies. Many times, one person plays the part of several of these roles. Often, that person is you, playing all of the parts, or at least trying to manage the cast of characters to the advantage of your child. Frequently, you as the parent juggle the conflicting roles of coach, parent, and caddy.

However, when it comes time for your child to tee it up in a junior tournament, only two roles really matter: those of the caddy and the player. There is no role of "parent," aside from extreme behavioral situations. There are also spectators, but they are the audience; not the actors.

It is the caddy's role that causes much of our parental angst, with our front-row seat to the golfing travails of our children. How difficult it is for us to stop parenting, stop criticizing, and second-guessing what our children do on the golf course! If only we could just watch, detached from the outcome, and enjoy seeing them play the game.

For a moment, put yourself in their shoes. Imagine yourself as a golfer playing in a big tournament, perhaps your club championship. You want a little help, so you hire a caddy. You want your caddy to be knowledgeable, respectful of you, and to help you play your best, right? So, when you tee off on the first hole and slice your drive out of bounds, how would you feel if he said something like "well, isn't that a great way to start! Opened your clubface and shanked it OB.

Didn't take long to ruin your round!"? I'm going to guess that his tenure as your caddy might be very brief.

Yet, that is frequently how it goes in the world of junior golf. Only with two exceptions – your child didn't hire you to be his caddy, and he can't fire you. He is stuck with you whether you do a good job or not. The truth is that you would probably be a much better caddy for someone else's child than you are for your own, if only because you would not act so much like a parent. There would be a lot more teamwork and a lot less dictating. And that is the crux of this chapter.

At the risk of oversimplifying, players have a very specific role and that is to play golf. Caddies also have a specific job to do – their job is to support the player at all times by being a good teammate. The player is king. The caddy is court jester. However, when parents and kids are involved, and emotions run high, and golf gets difficult (when isn't it?), these roles can easily become confused. Caddies morph back into parents. Kids forget they are golfers. Spectators intervene. Tears fall. Scores rise.

So let's take a clinical look at these roles and describe them. What should each do? When should they do it? Remember that the goal is to help the player perform at his or her best at all times. I believe that we caddy/parents are in the most powerful position to influence how our children play and how much fun they have with golf.

After all, we *are* the parents. Ironically, in order to get the kind of performance from our children that we really want, we have to give up some of our parental control and follow a new job description. If we take the lead, our children can follow and also give up some of their resistance to our parental controls and mature into their role as a golfer. For all of us daddy caddies, the sooner that happens, the better!

> **Caddy** (from Wikipedia):
>
> In golf, a **caddy** (or **caddie**) is the person who carries a player's bag and clubs, and gives insightful advice and moral support. A good caddy is aware of the challenges and obstacles of the golf course being played, along with the best strategy in playing it. This includes knowing overall yardage, pin placements, and club selection.

Your Job as Caddy

Watch a PGA Tour event sometime (in person, if possible), and watch closely what the caddy does. He carries a heavy bag and literally runs everywhere his player goes, all while picking up and replacing divots, retrieving dropped clubs, wiping the ball clean, giving perfect yardage and strategic advice, and pumping up his player's ego at every chance. Why does he do all of this? Because he likes his job, and he knows that his player is the boss. And, the better his player plays, the more money the caddy earns.

If you are to be your child's caddy, when you park your car at the golf course on tournament day your job as parent is over for a while. You are now the caddy, and your player is the boss (except perhaps for putting on sunscreen and holding a little one's hand for safety in the parking lot). Of course, the player has a few things to do in order to play his best, but don't worry... I'll address those things soon.

For now, however, it is your job to follow your player around, carrying his bag and doing his bidding for the next several hours. It might be difficult to become your child's as-

6

sistant, but that is the way it needs to work. If you hired me as his caddy, would you want me bossing him around and telling him what to do and how to do it?

Well, okay… don't answer that question. But really, this is a team effort, and the player is the team leader. Your job as caddy is supportive. Be 100% positive, supportive, and absorptive… as in absorbing all of the slings and arrows that will be hurled your way when someone (you) needs to be blamed for a bad shot.

Speaking of blame, the best golfers never make bad swings. The ball may not go where they want it to go, but at least to them, it isn't their fault. Golf is so difficult and so personal that it can be overwhelmingly self-defeating to the player to admit that he failed attempting a shot. It is much better to blame something or someone else and move on. That way the same type of shot can be attempted again later on without the memory of failure.

You are your player's sole teammate during competition, so you must do everything possible to help your player perform to his fullest potential. If that means accepting the blame for a missed putt ("it broke more than you thought, Dad"), then accept it. Swallow your parental pride and watch your player blossom.

Speaking of errors, as caddy you should not comment on a bad shot. More than anything, your junior golfer wants to please you, and hitting a bad shot makes him feel like he let you down. There is no need to call a bad shot bad. Your player knows it. He reacts more to your reaction than to the shot itself. In fact, it can even be dangerous to call a good shot good!

When I began my caddying job, I thought it best to keep things factual. When my son hit a poor shot, I called it for what it was. "Hooked that one," I'd say. To which he would quickly reply "no, the wind got it," or something of that nature. It seemed that no bad shot was his fault, and we constantly argued about what went wrong. So I got smart. I stopped commenting on bad shots and just gave positive support. "Nice shot," I'd say, or "that's okay, it's all right... no problem." Well, it took him about one nanosecond to come back with the opposite again. "How can you say that is okay?," or "it's not all right, it's in the rough." So, again we argued.

Then, I thought about my own experiences when I was a kid. My dad always complimented me and said "great shot," no matter what I thought about my shots. Nothing made me madder than hitting what I considered to be a poor shot and having him call it good. I expected more of myself, and I thought he should too. But how can we know what our children's expectations are? Our standards of good shots and bad shots may not match theirs.

The safest ground, then, is to keep your own interpretations to yourself, and try not to pass judgment. After all, a good shot to you might be a poor shot to someone else. But if you know your player's game well enough to really know what is good and bad to them then it is probably safe to offer up a compliment for obvious good shots. And it is definitely best to stay quiet in the wake of poor shots and simply move on. I'll get to the emotional management issues in chapter 3, but as caddy, your own emotions and opinions may be unwelcome and counter-productive.

The Caddy's Responsibilities

Now let's get down to the basics. As your child's caddy, what should you do? Consider the following job responsibilities, beginning with the easiest and moving on to the most valuable (to the player) and challenging (to you):

— Carry the player's bag wherever the player goes.

— Hand the player whatever club he or she wants, when he or she wants it.

— Clean said club and replace it in the player's bag after use.

Okay, I know this sounds silly so far, but your player might know more about his or her own game and capabilities than you do. He might just only need a pack mule, dad. In reality, however, every golfer needs some moral support also, so let's add a few more responsibilities:

— Say "good shot," "nice swing," or make some other positive comments at the right time.

— Know when to say nothing at all. Keep in mind that your body language speaks volumes, so avoid gestures, posturing, making faces, loud exhaling, throwing hands in the air, stomping around, looking at the sky, etc. True teammates don't do that stuff. Yes, you are mad about that poor shot. Yes, your player made an error. He didn't do it on purpose.

Don't make it worse! Help your player move on to the next shot and focus on what needs to be done from there.

— Make the player feel like a king or queen. Put him or her on a pedestal for a few hours. Everyone plays better golf when they feel good about themselves.

Well, so far, the caddy could be just about any supportive friend strong enough to tote the player's bag, and for some players, that could be enough. However, every golfer needs a sounding board for decision-making, so if you really want to add value to your team, let's list a few more:

— Know your player's shot making capabilities, meaning distances with every club, ability to control the ball's trajectory, curvature, direction, and distance. There is no room for braggadocio or grandstanding here. You need to know your player's <u>exact</u> carry yardages with each club, under a variety of lie scenarios (e.g., fairway, rough, bare lie, thick grass, etc.).

— Know the golf course — yardages, locations of hazards, boundaries, the architect's secret "gotchas" such as false green fronts, hidden bunkers, doglegs, sucker hole locations, etc. If you don't know these things ahead of time, you'll need to figure them out on the fly by watching others, glancing ahead at holes to be played that may be adjacent to you, and consulting the golf course's scorecard or yardage book if available. You might not be able to consult your friendly GPS handheld unless tournament rules permit their use, but you will usually be able to use a laser range finder as long as it doesn't measure changes in elevation.

— Based on the above, make recommendations or suggestions about club selection and shot strategy. Remember that your player must live with the outcome of his shot, so you are only making a *suggestion*. Let your player make the final decision, then say "that is the perfect club for you" and support him 100%. If it ends up being the wrong club, go ahead and take the blame. Maybe you misread the wind, or the lie wasn't as good as you thought, or it was more uphill, or you should have suggested a different club… you get the idea.

— Know how to read greens. Reading greens is a combination of art and science, and there are many books dedicated to the subject. Do some homework and help your player solve the 3D geometry. However, remember that the most important part of putting is distance control, so help your player figure the speed. And, when your player jams his ball ten feet past the hole, secretly clench your teeth, smile like it doesn't matter, and go help him line up the come-backer.

— Know the rules of golf well enough to help your player in certain situations, protect your player from mistakes, and protect the field from mistakes or violations by fellow competitors, especially the player whose scorecard your player is keeping. I'll cover some of the rules basics for caddies in chapter 2.

— Before the round, work with your player to develop a hole-by-hole strategy to take advantage of your player's strengths and minimize his weaknesses. This includes when to play it safe, when to be aggressive, thinking at least one shot ahead, and planning to leave the ball in the optimal location for the best approach to the green.

As you can see, the caddy has a difficult and important job. It isn't easy to swallow your pride, park your ego, and become an equal partner and teammate with your child. As parents we are accustomed to mandating and dictating orders to our children. As caddy, however, you will make recommendations and suggestions and provide factual information that your player can process and use to make his decisions. And, that is the beauty of it! Because, by so doing, your child will learn to collect information, make decisions, and be responsible for his or her actions. What could be better?

Player (sports) (from Roget's Thesaurus):

In sport, a **player** is a participant, team member, competitor, or contestant in an event.

The Player

In some ways, your child has the easiest job. All he has to do is play golf! After all, how hard can it be to concentrate and focus for a few hours while performing an extremely complicated task under changing conditions, with the pressure of performance expectations from himself and others, and under the microscopic watchful eye of parents, friends, and subject to the pressure from competitors?

Well... now that I think about it, let's give the player a break, because golf is the most difficult and demanding game in the world. It is a lot to ask of anyone, especially a young adult or a young child.

Still, the player has some distinct responsibilities. One of the most important of these is to be a good teammate together with his or her caddy. My son's school has a TEAM motto: **T**ogether **E**veryone **A**chieves **M**ore, and he and I use this motto in our golf. Virtually every poor shot or bad hole can be traced to some breakdown in teamwork. Teamwork problems include deviations from planned strategy, arguments over club selection, and any time the caddy and player disagree.

Your player needs to know that he is part of a team and, in fact, is the team leader. It takes time to learn how to work together productively, so take it slowly and don't expect instant results. Steady improvement is the goal. When you perform your caddy role as described earlier, you will gain his trust as a valuable partner and he will be better able to do his job making pars and birdies.

The player is responsible for his golf ball, and every decision that affects the ball's future should be made by the player. As difficult as it may be, the player should listen to his caddy's suggestions and recommendations and consider the facts. Smart players will use all available resources to help them make the best decisions, and to take good care of their golf ball.

However, in my experience, even smart children may not always make the smartest decisions on (and off!) the golf course. When this happens, the final decision regarding club selection and shot strategy must still be made by the player, and he is responsible for the result. Again, this is where you say "that sounds perfect," and hope for the best. And please, no "I told you so" comments if the shot doesn't come off as planned.

But I may be getting ahead of myself. The player has a lot of work to do to prepare for tournament play, and some specific things to do while playing and afterwards. Here's a list:

— Develop goals. Nothing breeds success like goals, because goals come from dreams, and dreams provide the inspiration to achieve almost anything. Walt Disney said "if you can dream it, you can do it," and that motto applies directly to golf. Help your child begin with a dream and write down his goals. It is extremely important that he write them down, because something magical will happen when he sees those words on paper. The words come alive, and they serve as his motivation and inspiration to practice and work to achieve his goals.

Now, keep in mind that I am not suggesting that your child's goals be so lofty or far-fetched that they remain only dreams. He may dream of breaking 40 for nine holes. He may dream of winning a local tournament, or finishing in the top 20 in a national event. He may dream of playing nine holes without a 3-putt, or of keeping his score below triple-bogey on each hole. Goals can be successive stepping stones that carry him forward as he progresses and his game improves. And, they can be revised as needed to reflect his improvement. As an example, my son Alex set his goals for the 2012 U.S. Kids World Championships as follows:

1. Be a great team

2. Finish in the top 5

He and I both knew that he would play his best if we focused on teamwork. We also knew that if we did not work together as a team, his finish would be irrelevant. Notice that at no point above have I said anything at all about *your* goals as the parent. Yes, you want him to be on the PGA Tour someday. Of course you want him to earn that college scholarship. But, this is not about you (sorry to be so blunt). These dreams and goals must be those of your child. Put your own desires on the shelf and let him dream a bit, and then help him develop goals that can get him there.

–   Develop a plan. Your child's dream and his goals will not come to fruition without some work. He needs a plan that addresses his practice regimen and provides competitive opportunities. This is where parent and player work together to decide practice schedules, lesson frequency, and to map out the calendar with available tournament opportunities. As an example, in my case, I worked with my son and we developed the following plan according to what he wanted to do:

1. Attend golf camp and play/practice as much as possible with peers in an informal, fun setting. Productive practice does not have to be work!

2. Play in as many local competitions as possible, subject to our schedules.

3. Improve distance by building strength. He also loves baseball, so we frequented the batting cages, and we began some very simple exercises using his body weight (sit-ups, push-ups, pull-ups, etc.). No, I don't think baseball swings are bad for golf swings, and swinging a bat can really help build club-head speed.

4. Focus on approach shots from 40 yards and under, aiming to get them closer to the hole and produce more birdie opportunities.

5. Practice distance control on long putts.

6. Practice making those 3-4 footers.

— Implement the plan. Your child has his dream, has developed a goal, and has a practice plan to get there. The only thing left is to do it. It is the player's ultimate responsibility to do his best to prepare for competition; to bring his best game to the first tee.

That will not happen without practice and preparation according to his plan.

All of the above brings us to the player's one and only job on tournament day – to play golf. As I mentioned, your player needs to be prepared to play his best. Here are some suggested responsibilities for your player prior to and on tournament day:

– Meet with his caddy and discuss the golf course, and develop a playing strategy for each hole. This can be done during a practice round or, if you know the course well, in casual conversation. The point here is for your player to buy in to the strategy in cases where less than full tee shots, layups, or other care is needed... before standing on the tee and debating what to do in the tournament. This also minimizes the chances of being negatively influenced by what other players may do during the round. Your player should stick to his game plan, since it was developed as a team and should provide the best opportunity for him to post a good score.

– Get enough sleep the night before the tournament.

– Eat a healthy breakfast the morning of the event (keep sugars to a minimum).

– Get to the golf course at least one hour, but not more than 90 minutes, ahead of his tee time. I find one hour to be perfect. This doesn't mean pulling in to the parking lot one hour ahead; it means being checked in and on the putting green one hour ahead of his tee time. Leave extra time for finding that parking space, putting on golf shoes, lathering up with sunscreen, figuring out how to unfold that pull-cart, etc. Also leave extra time if the golf course logistics are poor, such as a practice range or first tee that is far from the clubhouse.

— Look his caddy in the eye, do a big "high 5" and leave the car with the goal to be great teammates for the next several hours.

— After check-in, go straight to the putting green and get used to the speed. Start by practicing long putts, trying to lag them close (within 3 feet) to the hole. Practice uphill and downhill putts. Hit a few chip shots to get used to the firmness of the greens and how the ball bounces and rolls.

— Get to the driving range by 40 minutes from tee time, and warm up with short pitch shots, short irons, and full swings, working up to the driver. Your player shouldn't hit more than 10 balls with any club, and should use only 4-5 clubs. Remember, it is warm-up time. This is not the time to work on your player's golf swing. At this late hour, it is what it is, and your player will need to do his best with his game as-is. Your job as caddy here is to tell your player how wonderful his swing is, and how great he looks. Come on... a little white lie doesn't hurt... help him get rid of any nerves or doubts and just swing freely.

- With 20 minutes to go, head back to the putting green and work on long and short putts. Again, the emphasis should be on distance control, practicing both uphill and downhill putts if the green allows. Your player should also putt those testy 3-4 footers, but if they are not going in, don't worry about it. Have him hit some shorter putts to get the ball into the hole and to bolster his confidence. This is no time to struggle and go to the course with bad memories of missing short putts.

- With 10 minutes to go, get to the first tee starter, listen to any special instructions for the event, meet and greet your fellow competitors, and take a few practice swings. Get together as a caddy – player team, promise to have fun no matter what, give each other another big "high 5," and tee it up.

- While on the course, your player must remember to be a team player, and treat his caddy as an equal teammate. Your player is going to be making decisions on shot strategy and club selection, but you will have plenty of suggestions for him to consider. Your player should consider your suggestions, thank you for the advice, and make his decision. And, he should try not to place too much blame on his poor hapless caddy if his ball doesn't behave nicely. No matter what happens, your player needs to respect you and your position as caddy… and you need to respect him and how hard he is trying to do his best.

—   Your player is going to hit some bad shots out there. Everybody does. That bad shot won't be the end of the world, but it could launch a tsunami of more bad shots if he lets it. Don't let that happen. Help him to be confident, believe in himself, shrug off bad shots, remember the good shots, and see this as a challenge to get back on track. I'll discuss this topic more later.

—   Your player needs to pay attention to the other players in the group, and help keep track of their scores. He can have fun and talk with them, but must get serious and focus when it is time for him to hit. In my experience, there is approximately a 100% chance that your player's next shot will not be a good one if he is goofing around right before hitting. There is a place for goofing around, but it isn't on the golf course. Great players have a way of switching from relaxed mode (between shots) to focused mode for the next shot. I'll address this topic in more detail in chapter 3.

—   When your player has completed his round, he needs to sign his scorecards (one as marker for another player and his own card as the player). When that is done and you have exited the scoring area, smile a lot. Tell him to hug his mom and dad – after all, now you aren't caddy and spectator any more! Let him goof around a bit. He *is* still a kid!

Spectator (from Roget's Thesaurus):

In sport, a **spectator** is an observer, a bystander, an outsider and a witness to an event.

Spectators and Others

My handy thesaurus says that a spectator is an observer, a bystander, an outsider and a witness to an event. Even though you may be the parent or a relative, that is an accurate description of your role as a spectator in a tournament. Spectators should remain away from the action, secluded in the rough or on the cart path. You should try to minimize your influence on your child and allow him to be himself and play his own game.

This isn't as easy as it sounds. Never underestimate your power, even from under the tree behind the 4th green where you thought you were hiding out of sight. When your child misses that short putt, he will first look straight at you to get your reaction. Be stoic, or at most, show him that it is okay by pretending you didn't even see it. This is no time for showing disappointment, throwing hands in the air, yelling instructions, shaking heads, or any other body language. Show him that it doesn't really matter whether that putt went in or not. What matters is how he handles the setback and that he goes forward with his best game from that point.

Spectators should not become involved in rules questions and should not communicate with the player during play. Spectators should cheer players and applaud good shots, but do so with caution and respect to other players on nearby holes who may be distracted.

Golf is not baseball, soccer, or football, and there is no place for vocal cheering or other stadium behavior. Think of how you would act while watching your child's piano recital or perhaps a spelling bee. You watch quietly, dying inside, taking too many pictures and videos, hanging on his every move, praying for the best. So it is and should be with golf.

One very important role that you can play as a spectator for younger players is transportation. Although players are required to walk during the play of a hole, they may usually be transported from a green to the next tee. That is the time to give your child an ego boost, some water, a snack, and help him focus on his next shot, forgetting any past transgressions. This is definitely <u>not</u> the time to discuss swing mechanics or any other golf issues. Give your player a break and allow him to relax and regroup for the rest of his round.

The Parent

With the exception of unusual circumstances that might involve disciplinary or other requirements such as bathroom breaks, the parent has no role to play on the golf course during a tournament other than as a spectator. Leave your parent hat in the car and bring out the pom-poms. This advice applies to non-caddying parents and other family members. You are spectators on the golf course, and cheerleaders for your child. There will be plenty of time to parent after the round.

The Coach

Your player's coach could be a PGA/LPGA professional, a dedicated golf coach, or another person acting as coach. Or, you may be his coach. There is an enormous role played by coaches in developing your player's golf game. However, at this time during a tournament, unless the coach is also the caddy, the coach is relegated to the role of spectator, subject to all of the spectator guidelines above. I'll discuss the coach's role extensively in chapters 4-7, whether played by you or someone else.

Caddy / Player Side-By-Side –
A Typical Tournament Play-by-Play Analysis

Since most of the previous discussion has centered on your role as caddy and your player's responsibilities, it may be helpful to summarize them together as they may occur on a tournament day. The following table brings caddy and player together and shows how the team should work.

Where / When	Daddy Caddy	Player
Pre Tournament	Help player develop goals. Assist player in preparation of practice plan (work with a PGA/ LPGA professional or coach as needed) • Physical • Mental • Scrambling • Long Putts • Approach Shots • Tee Shots	Write goals on paper – own them Prepare plan to achieve goals Implement plan
On Arriving at Golf Course	Carry player's golf clubs anywhere he or she goes	**Focus on goals**
Warm Up	Give player confidence and positive feedback about his shotmaking skills	**Be ready to play** Get feel for greens (speed and firmness for putting and chipping) Test bunker sand Loosen up swing and be ready with best possible game from the 1st tee on
On the Tee	Know the golf course and your player's capabilities Offer recommendations and suggestions on playing strategy	**Decide Strategy** Know your own strengths and capabilities Listen to suggestions from your caddy

Where / When	Daddy Caddy	Player
Before Hitting a Shot	Provide accurate distance measurements to targets Suggest club selection strategy	**Select club** Know your own club distances under a wide variety of situations (quality of lie, slopes, wind, temperature, etc.)
Pre-Shot Routine	Help player remain focused on the shot at hand, not on overall score or what any other player may be doing	**Hit the shot** Use a consistent pre-shot routine. Make best effort to hit a good shot
Post Shot	Celebrate success / ignore failure Help player stay loose and energized between shots; discuss non-golf topics and create a relaxing environment	**Stay cool** Keep a positive attitude and forget the past (bad shots, mistakes, etc.)… but, remember the good shots!
Immediate Post Round	Congratulate player on accomplishments: • Finishing the round • Being a team player • Remember good shots • Having fun	Verify and sign scorecard. Thank your caddy for his/her help
Later (Next Day) Post Round	Review round and discuss opportunities for improvement. What were your player's strengths and weaknesses? Ask player to review practice plan and assist with suggestions for any changes.	Keep an open mind to discussion about strengths, weaknesses, and opportunities for improvement. Review practice plan and modify as needed

•   •   •

The best way to summarize this chapter may be to say that sometimes, the simplest things are the most difficult to do. It is easy to wear one hat at a time, but not so easy to avoid switching hats every minute or so. Not to minimize its complexity, but being a caddy is not so hard if that is all you try to do. However, it is quite difficult to stop being a daddy! As impossible as that is, we still need to pretend and do a bit of role-playing when we are on the bag. While caddying... be a caddy and follow the job description outlined in this chapter. The less you act like a parent the more effective you will be, and the better your child will behave.

That is why my best advice might be to pretend that you are caddying for someone else's child. I'll go out on a limb and predict that you would both be more respectful of each other. You would be more tolerant of the other child's mistakes. And, your role would be much more supportive and encouraging. Yes, your child knows how to push your buttons in a way that another player wouldn't. Yes, he is learning the game and about himself, as are you. But he is trying his best, and he only wants to please you.

And players... pretend like you have a PGA Tour caddy on the bag. Yes, your Daddy Caddy is far from ready to be on tour, and he is learning this process as are you. But he is also trying his best and he only wants you to succeed.

CHAPTER TWO

"There are 34 rules of golf... and it only takes a 181 page rules book plus a 752 page 'decisions' book to explain them!"

The Rules of Golf... for the Caddy

Many people think that the rules of golf are too complicated. For certain, there are many nuances to the rules that can be confusing or lead to misinterpretations. However, at its core, I think golf is played by one simple principle: start and finish each hole with the same ball, playing it as it lies until you remove it from the hole. Most of the rules of golf have evolved to help you handle situations when this fundamental concept is impractical (e.g., you don't want to play your ball from where it lies inside that bush) or impossible (e.g., your ball is at the bottom of a lake or in someone's back yard).

To my knowledge, golf is the only sport where the participants police themselves. Thus, integrity and honesty are integral elements of the game, as is trust that others share and abide by those same values.

Because there are no referees or umpires, you need to be familiar with the USGA Rules of Golf. Get the book from the USGA or your local golf shop, read it, and keep it in your child's golf bag at all times. I can't include those rules in this book, but I can offer some advice with a few situations that frequently become problems, especially with junior golfers and their caddies. Rules issues can become discussions that can escalate into heated arguments. Your knowledge of the rules will help avoid uncomfortable situations.

When disagreements do occur, and when it is necessary for a player to be penalized, remember that it is not *you* who are penalizing someone. An impartial way out is to say something like "let's see what the USGA has to say about this," and look it up in your rules book.

Also, you should know that in cases where it is one player's word against another, the rules committee will side with the player unless there is a third party witness to the event. When there is a genuine difference of opinion and a rules official is not available for consultation, the best approach is for the affected player to play a second ball. There is a very specific procedure for doing this, so refer to the USGA rule book and make sure to announce which ball your player wants to count if the rules allow.

Golf is a game of honor, and it is the player's responsibility to understand the rules and call violations on himself. We all have to live with our own conscience, and if a rules violation happens to your player, you and he will both know it. Each rules issue becomes a valuable life lesson for your child in being honest and making the right decision.

Another reason to be rules savvy is to be able to help your player avoid mistakes and penalties. You also have the responsibility to help protect the rest of the field from a player who might gain some advantage by violating a rule, whether through ignorance or intention. This means that if you witness a rules violation, you have the responsibility to call it on the player who committed the violation. If you ignore violations, you are giving that player an unfair advantage against the remainder of the field.

If you are faced with a rules question, make sure to deal with it immediately, or no later than the conclusion of the hole being played. If you wait until the scoring area when the round is over, memories will have faded and the exact circumstances will be difficult to recall and agree upon.

Given the importance of the rules, let's expand on your role as caddy with a few more responsibilities.

— **Count his clubs** — Make sure that there are no more than 14 clubs in his bag before he tees off on the first hole. It is easy to leave one of your own clubs in the bag from yesterday's practice session, or forget that he was trying that extra driver or that new putter. Count his clubs before each round and avoid a needless penalty.

— **Keep Score** — When you caddy for your child, you will usually find yourself keeping score for another competitor in your group. This simple-sounding task can become quite difficult when things go awry and that player swings away with little result. It is your player's job, and thus yours, to keep track of things and count each stroke. There is absolutely no substitute for announcing each player's score and agreeing BEFORE you walk off the putting green on each hole. That way, if there is any difference of opinion, it can be resolved when memories are fresh.

— **Play Quickly** – Let's face it: slow play is the bane of golf, especially tournament golf. In fact, slow play is one of the most common reasons people give for not enjoying the game. You can do your part to prevent slow play by helping your player be ready to play when it is his turn. This means paying attention to other players and knowing whose ball is farthest from the hole at all times. It is irrelevant whether or not a ball is on the green when determining order of play. The only thing that matters is distance from the hole.

Being ready to play also means that your player should make strategic and club selection decisions while other players are doing their business. Don't wait until it is his turn to play before measuring yardages, determining the wind speed, tossing grass clippings into the air, surveying the green, taking the air temperature, making practice swings, and so on.

I am not suggesting that your player rush when it is his turn to play. Quite the contrary. He should go through his normal pre-shot routine and not feel hurried. However, much of the time consuming business can be done while fellow competitors are playing their shots, so that your player is ready to focus on the shot and begin his routine when it is his turn.

If you and your player have developed a complex pre-shot routine that involves your guidance and direction on aim, stance, posture, ball position, hand position, and another 5-point checklist, your child is going to gain a reputation as a slow player. I highly recommend that you work with him to eliminate his reliance on you for this pre-shot agony.

Your role should be more strategic, involving target and shot selection and acting less like a puppeteer. This is another chance to allow your child to be responsible for his own shot outcome. The sooner you can get away from over-coaching, the better he will play and the less you will be blamed for the outcome of the shot.

If your group does fall behind the group in front, each player may be subject to a penalty for slow play. Therefore, it is imperative to pay attention to the group in front of yours and keep up with them throughout the round.

— **Watch your player's and your fellow competitor's balls so you can prevent problems with:**

o **Wrong ball** – Don't let your player make the mistake of playing a wrong ball. Watch where the ball goes, and double-check its markings before your player hits his next shot. Speaking of markings, your player's ball must always be marked uniquely so that it can be identified. It is not enough that his ball is a different brand or number from that of others in his group. His ball must be marked with an indelible marker. Let him have some fun and mark it according to his personality, using colors or designs of his choosing.

o **Out of bounds** – Even though you would probably rather cover your eyes or look away, watch closely if your player's ball goes off line. If your player's ball goes out of bounds he must re-play the stroke from the ball's previous location, and add a one-stroke penalty. It can take a long time to search for the ball, discover that it is "OB," walk back to the spot from which the previous shot was played and then hit the shot again. It can even subject your player to a slow play penalty if his group falls behind due to these delays.

Avoid this problem by playing a "provisional ball" if you think your player's ball may be out of bounds or lost outside of a water hazard (he cannot play a provisional ball if his ball might be lost in a water hazard).

If he intends to play a provisional ball, make sure he announces that fact and uses a ball with different markings before hitting the ball. If he fails to call that ball a "provisional ball," the original ball must be abandoned even if it is later found in bounds.

o **Lost ball** – As with a ball out of bounds, a lost ball requires your player to go back and replay the previous shot. Watching the ball as it flies can prevent delays and penalties in case the ball can't be found. The same provisional ball procedure applies if you think his ball may be lost outside of a water hazard.

o **Water hazard entry point** – Fortunately, many tournaments feature "drop zones" for balls that go in a water hazard that requires a forced carry over the water. You should be informed about the existence of drop zones by the starter on the first tee, or by a local rules sheet. If there isn't a drop zone, you need to know your player's drop options for water hazards, which can be a bit complicated.

The most important thing to know is where the ball last crossed the margin of the hazard. You need to know the differences between lateral water hazards (red stakes) and "regular" water hazards (yellow stakes). Consult the USGA Rules of Golf book for detailed information on dropping options.

o **Ball moved at address** – Young junior golfers have an unfortunate tendency to accidently bump the ball with their clubhead before making their swing. Unfortunately, unless the ball is on the tee, this can result in a series of penalties worth one or two strokes: one stroke for moving the ball and one additional stroke for failing to replace it before playing the next shot. If the ball is accidentally moved, inform your fellow competitors and replace it. Then, add one penalty stroke.

When this happens on the putting green, your player may be anxious to hit the putt and forget to move the ball back. Add another penalty stroke, for a total of two (only the more severe two-stroke penalty applies). Most important, make sure you know what "move" means according to the rules. A ball that simply rocks back and forth (or "oscillates") has not moved. For a ball to move, it must leave its place and end up in a different place.

o **Teeing ground** – One of the simplest concepts in golf is to begin each hole from within the teeing ground, which is bounded in front by a straight line connecting the two tee markers. Occasionally, another player will inadvertently tee his ball in front of the markers.

If you notice this, let the other player know immediately so they can move it back behind the markers before they hit. This is good golf etiquette and will avoid a tense, anger-filled conversation as to how this two-stroke penalty could have been avoided. And, for your player, make sure the ball is behind the markers. One foot behind won't cost him the tournament or make the hole play any longer.

– **Take care with advice to your player and fellow competitors**:

o **Distances** – If you are the only lucky one in the group to have a laser rangefinder, you will be able to determine your player's exact yardage to various features of the golf course. If your fellow competitors do not have a distance measuring device, the rules allow them to ask you for distance information between any two objects, including their ball and the hole. As a matter of good golf etiquette, you should provide that information if asked. After doing so, you may also kindly suggest that they get their own rangefinder!

If you do intend to use a distance measuring device, make sure it does not provide other information such as change in elevation or slope and wind speed. Most tournament rules prohibit the use of rangefinders that have these capabilities.

o **Club selection** – As a guideline, do not discuss club selection with other players before hitting. It is a rules violation for your player to tell a fellow competitor what club he is using, and it is a violation to ask someone else what club they are using. However, it is not a violation to look at a fellow competitor's club and see what club it is. It is even permissible to look into the other player's bag to see what club is missing, unless they have covered their clubs with a towel or something to prevent you from peeking.

o **Aligning your player** – Another kind of advice to your player is aiming advice, or alignment. As the caddy, you are allowed to stand behind your player and help him aim his club and position his body. However, you must not remain on the target line behind your player while he plays his shot, or you will cost him two extra strokes.

This is one of the most frequently violated rules, usually due to lack of knowledge. I advise against aligning your player to begin with... it is one more opportunity for him to make his own decisions and become independent and responsible for his golf ball. If you aim him, I can almost guarantee that whatever happens will be blamed on you. However, if you "must" aim your player, move well away from the aiming line before he or she swings.

— **Keep your player and yourself away from the ball before playing the shot**. It is tempting to go up to the ball, poke around a bit, and take a few swings to test the grass around the ball. Stay away or your player will likely be blamed in the event the ball decides to nestle further down into the rough. At a minimum, other players will wonder what you and your player are doing around the ball, and it may appear that the lie of the ball is being improved

  o **Loose impediments** (not including sand or dirt) – You can remove things like leaves, twigs, rocks, and other natural things that are no longer fixed or growing… but make sure it can be done without moving the ball (see ball moved above). You may brush away sand or dirt lying on the putting green, but elsewhere it cannot be touched.

  o **Obstructions** – Artificial objects can be either moveable (e.g., a soda can) or immoveable (e.g., a sprinkler head or a paved cart path). Either way, your player can take free relief by either moving the ball or the obstruction. But – and this is very important – look around before picking the ball

THE RULES OF GOLF... FOR THE CADDY

up and know where your player will be dropping when he takes relief, because that place might just be worse than where the ball originally lay. Once he picks up the ball, he is required to take up to one club length from the nearest point of relief (not closer to the hole), even if that point is in the middle of bushes. Notice the wording: "nearest point of relief." Your player must find the place nearest to where his ball lies that is not closer to the hole and that would provide relief (both stance and swing) from the obstruction. He is not entitled to a "nice" place; only the nearest.

o **Practice swings**, if taken too close to the ball, can result in a "ball moved" penalty. Use caution, especially in long grass or pine needles, where even a practice swing taken a few feet away from the ball can cause the ball to move. I do recommend that your player take swings to test the grass or other conditions that will affect the next shot. However, this should be done in similar conditions at least two club lengths away from the ball.

– **Take care on the putting green**:

o **Indicating line of putt** (touching the green) – When you and your player are reading the green, you will want to point out an aiming spot to allow for the putt to break. No problem there… but don't touch the surface of the green. Just point.

o **Ball marks vs. spike or scuff marks** – It is a rules violation to fix scuff marks or other imperfections on the putting green, except for marks made by a ball landing on the green. When in doubt, simply ask your fellow competitors for their opinion and go with it. It is a real bummer to see a "mountain" on the green between your player's ball and the hole, but it probably isn't a ball mark, so don't touch it without asking. If your player accidently scuffs his or her feet on the green, make sure to repair the marks after everyone has putted out on the hole.

o **Testing the surface** – Have you ever tried to pet a cat from tail to head? It doesn't work, because the "grain" of its fur runs the other way. Putting greens have grain, but don't try to rub the surface to find in which direction it runs. You can usually see the grain by looking closely at the hole. The edge of the hole will be worn on the side toward which the grain is running. You may also notice that when you look across the green, the grass may look either shiny or dull. If it is shiny, you are looking with the grain and a putt in that direction will roll faster than a putt in the other direction. Discuss these observations with your player while you are sizing up his putt, and remember that rubbing the surface of the green will cost your player two strokes.

o **Marking and replacing the ball** – You and your player may be teammates for the competition, but you are not partners according to the rules of golf. Therefore, you cannot interchangeably mark and replace a ball on the putting green. Although you are allowed to mark and lift your player's ball, he or she must authorize you to do it *each time*. No blanket authorization is allowed. The best practice is to avoid any confusion and a needless penalty by always having your player mark and replace his ball. Plus, that is another area of personal responsibility that your player should have. He, not you, is in control of his golf ball.

— **Know about relief options**. Throughout the course of his round, your player may encounter situations where his ball needs to be lifted and moved in accordance with the rules. Know these rules! They are fairly simple, but it is easy to make a mistake. These areas include:

o **Ground Under Repair** – This is an area usually marked by white paint on the ground that is being worked on by the greens crew or which is deemed to be "under repair." Your player can either play the ball from here (unless the area is a flower bed or something protected by local rules) or get a free drop.

o **Obstructions** – I mentioned obstructions earlier, and a free drop is usually in order, but not required. Your player can hit a shot from the paved cart path if he so chooses.

- **Casual Water** – Puddles following a rainstorm are called "casual water," and your player will get a free drop in the nearest dry area that isn't closer to the hole. But, use some caution here, as large wet areas may exist that might require dropping far away into a less desirable location. And, be careful with the definition of "casual water." A wet area is not automatically an abnormal ground condition under the rules. Check the definition in your USGA Rules of Golf book. As always, think about where the ball is going to be dropped *before* picking it up, because once it is lifted, it must be dropped away from the condition that caused your player to lift it.

- **Unplayable Lie** – Next to that root, lodged in a bush, or in thick trees with no chance to swing, your player's ball might just be unplayable. There are several drop options here, so consult your rules book and do the smart thing. It is so tempting to flail away at a ball in the thick stuff, but it might be better to just take the stroke penalty and drop safely away.

- **Lift, Clean, and Place** – Also known as "lift, clean, and cheat," this is a temporary local rule usually enacted due to extremely wet conditions. You will be informed of this by the starter or by the local rules sheet for the day (this rule might differ from day to day). You will be allowed to mark the ball's position (in the fairway only), lift it, clean off the mud, and place it back in a nice, cushy spot close to its original location (usually one scorecard length away). This is a huge advantage, and it is important for your player to keep his ball in the fairway to take advantage of this rule, since it doesn't apply to balls in the rough. Just remember that if you are going to do the lifting, your player needs to authorize you to do so each time.

— **Take care in hazards**. There are two types of hazards: bunkers and water, and they are both hazardous to your player's score. Your player should use extreme caution when playing a ball from a hazard, because it is easy to inadvertently violate a rule and incur a two-stroke penalty:

 o **Touching the sand in a bunker** – Your player's club cannot touch or brush any sand or loose impediment during the pre-shot or backswing. And, if your player unfortunately fails to extract his ball from the bunker and slams his club into the sand in exasperation... add two strokes.

 o **Grounding the club or touching loose impediments in a water hazard** – When your player's ball is within the margin of a water hazard, the ball might be playable if it is not actually under water. That could be great luck, but your player

41

cannot ground his club or touch the water or any loose impediments inside the hazard on his backswing. It might just be impossible to hit the ball without violating this rule, so think carefully before deciding to play a ball from within a hazard. It is okay it the club lightly touches grass or other vegetation that is alive (i.e., not a loose impediment).

• • •

As you can see, there are plenty of rules pitfalls, so you and your player should both study the rules of golf. Your knowledge of the rules will save your player strokes. Also, you should set an example by using good etiquette and demonstrating integrity. If you are respectful of other players and of the game, your child will learn to do the same. And if your child has a rules issue, demonstrate the highest integrity by calling the penalty yourself. There may be no greater life lesson he could learn.

This chapter is a simple overview of rules issues that you should know in your job as caddy. This overview is no substitute for reading and understanding the USGA's Rules of Golf. Even though they can seem complicated, there are only 34 rules of golf. You and your player should both become familiar with the rules so that you will know how to handle the rules-related situations that are guaranteed to arise.

As you study the rules, keep in mind the following advice to help simplify the process and focus on the most common rules-related situations:

- Even though there are 34 rules, most situations will arise from only 16 rules. Study these first as you work through the book:

  o #8 – Advice and Indicating Line of Play
  o #11-15 – Playing the ball
  o #18-28 – Ball moved and relief situations.

- Make sure you are not standing behind your player on or near the line of play while he or she plays a stroke, whether putting or hitting full shots.

- If you must lift your player's ball for some reason, always ask your player for permission first.

- Understand the USGA's "get out of jail free" rule known as Rule 3-3: Doubt as to Procedure. If you are not sure what to do, this rule allows your player to play a second ball and get a ruling later. However, there is a very specific process for doing this, so read the rule to avoid procedural problems.

CHAPTER THREE

*"It isn't so important that your child has game.
It is what he does with his game that matters."*

Managing the Mental Game

There are dozens of books and more websites devoted to the mental side of playing golf, written by psychiatrists and psychologists who know much more about how our brains work than I do. I encourage you to explore and research this fascinating topic. My favorite golf books are listed in the appendix and many of them provide excellent information that can help you understand the emotional challenges inherent in golf. Meanwhile, here is my layman's perspective on managing emotions on the golf course.

Golf is surely one of the most challenging games ever conjured up by humans. In no more than three hours, a typical golfer can experience virtually every emotion, from anger to jubilation to sadness to fear to embarrassment to satisfaction… and beyond. Hitting that first tee shot can fill us with performance anxiety surpassing even that felt giving a public speech. When your child hits a poor shot, he will feel anger and frustration, and we caddies feel it vicariously. Golf will test us all by providing our lowest of lows and our highest of highs. It is a lot to expect of anyone, much less a child, to maintain composure and manage themselves through such emotional turmoil.

Even when they play well, most golfers are dissatisfied with their performance. Coming off the ninth green after shooting a phenomenal 31 against a par of 36, one junior golfer was quick to tell me how much better she could have scored had she only made those three short putts! I think it is the golfer's curse. No matter how well we play, we always believe we should have done just a little better, if only that putt had gone in, or if that tee shot hadn't gone just a yard too far into the rough, or if only the wind hadn't been blowing, or the sun shining too brightly, or the earth spinning so rapidly. You get the idea.

Many times, we can sense our potential when we hit a shot perfectly. I jokingly tell my students, "if only you hadn't hit that one perfect shot, you could just quit playing golf and live a much more peaceful life." But we do hit those perfect shots just often enough to create hope and the promise of more of them. And we keep coming back for more, because golf gets inside us and challenges our very core. It gets personal. Golf creates the ultimate internal battle between good and evil. Golf exposes our true nature more quickly and purely than any other activity I know. You will learn more about someone in nine holes of golf than you will learn in years as their best friend.

> Watch any caddy while his child is hitting a shot. He will flinch noticeably at impact, as though he himself were hitting the ball. We all do… it is as though we are one in spirit with our child, and our emotions are linked through the ball and club into his or her soul.

One thing you can count on is that your child will hit a poor shot or two every time he plays. We all do. Even expert

PGA Tour players hit poor shots. Remember how you felt the last time you chunked a ball into the water, skulled one over the green, or 3-putted from five feet? Your child feels even more frustrated.

Like you, he feels that sense of failure and the belief that his round is now ruined. Plus, he is embarrassed in front of his friends. More importantly, he feels he has let you down, and he probably thinks you are going to be plenty mad at him for messing things up. As difficult as it is for us mature adults to manage our emotions, it is even more difficult for our children.

Keeping Up With the Joneses

Another thing you can count on is that your child will change his playing strategy, his swing, or his attitude in response to what the other players in his group are doing. We all do it. The other guy tees off first and hammers a shot 300 yards down the middle of the fairway. We think we need to do something to keep up – to live up to his standards, or to avoid the embarrassment of hitting a short or crooked tee shot.

So we change something. We swing harder or try a risky shot that we haven't done in practice or that we simply can't hit. It is incredibly difficult not to play someone else's game. And, it isn't made any easier by the requirement to pay attention to the others in the group so balls can be found and scores attested to.

> *No matter what the others are doing, stay the course and play the course.*

Although your player needs to pay attention to the other players, he (and you) must do everything possible to ignore what those players are doing and focus instead on playing his own game against the golf course. It is your child vs. "old man par." When your child feels inferior and tries to keep up with another player, he will change his game for the worse. Again, it comes down to managing his emotions.

These emotions can include embarrassment and self-directed anger due to real or perceived failure. Whether real or perceived, the effect on your player's performance is real. He may be sad about the way he is playing, and feel like he can't recover from a previous bad hole or two. He could be happy about a great shot or a birdie. He may be afraid that he won't keep playing well after a run of good holes, or that he won't finish well. All of these emotions, whether good or bad, can have a profound influence on your child's ability to perform at his best. In golf, as in life, we need to control ourselves and stay cool in the face of both adversity and good fortune.

Living Up to Expectations

Even though he may not show it, your child feels the pressure of expectations. He has his own standards of performance that he wants to live up to. And, he certainly is aware of your standards, either from your explicit statements or merely from subconscious suggestions you may have made.

Many times this pressure begins in the build-up to a tournament, when we innocently say something hoping to boost his confidence. You might be happy that his next tournament will be at his home course, and remark that this week should be easy, since he knows the course so well. Or, you might remind him of how much he has improved lately, and suggest that he will have a great round this week. Or, you might say something about "playing better this time," or "beating so-and-so this time."

When you compare your child to another player, you set up an invalid one-on-one comparison and increase the pressure to perform according to what he or she believes is your level of expectation. Such comparisons are invalid because, unless it is match play, golf is your player against the course. That other player could have a bad day and your child could beat them, only to find himself likewise beaten by several others in the field who weren't even on the radar.

As parents we can help minimize the pressure of expectations on our children by saying as little as possible, and by reminding them to keep it fun and enjoy the tournament experience.

Anger Management: Let 1 = 1

Someone once said that playing golf is a great idea when you are mad at someone else, because the game will make you so mad at yourself that you will forget all about the transgressions of others. Golf creates anger and frustration because we believe that we should be able to control our bodies and repeat a swing and an outcome that we have done before. When it doesn't happen, we feel as though we have failed, and our failure is exposed to all of those around us.

One key difference between good players and great players is the great ones can manage their emotions, control their anger, and as I say, "let 1 = 1." This means to let one bad shot cost you only one stroke (or less)… not more than one stroke. A junior golfer's tournament scorecard will usually show the carnage that unfolds after a mental meltdown, and it usually lasts for at least two holes. First there is the mistake: an unexpected hook into the water. Then the meltdown where all sense and reason evaporate in favor of random actions without conscious thought.

Then, a few more poor shots follow (it is not easy to hit a ball that is distorted by tears). The aftermath continues on the next tee, and for a few more shots until he can relax, having already ruined his score and having nothing more at stake.

It all comes down to anger management, and it is probably too much to expect for a young golfer to be able to recognize what is happening and regain control before all is lost. Therefore, you need to be the calm voice of reason. You also need to have a trick or two up your sleeve to help your player recover.

You need to recognize that anger is an emotional state that adversely affects our body chemistry and our ability to control our muscles. Anger makes it difficult to make our normal golf swing. Anger invades our mental processes and makes it almost impossible to think clearly and rationally.

What's worse, anger is extremely difficult to control once it has begun, and it tends to escalate before your child can finally calm down. Because anger alters our body chemistry, there may be nothing you can do to restore sanity and rational thought until the anger subsides. Thus, it is important to act quickly and head off the angry reaction before it escalates.

The first step in controlling your child's anger is recognition. You will see it coming before anyone, when a simple putt is missed or a bad swing sends his ball into trouble.

When this happens, here are a few actions he can take to derail the anger before it takes over:

- He should acknowledge his feelings, say "I'm angry" to himself and recognize what is happening. It is his anger that is the enemy, and he can defeat it.

- He should tell himself that he is not going to allow anger to grow inside him, and that anger is not going to ruin his round.

- He should not fight or suppress his feelings, because anger needs to be released.

- He should release the anger by taking a deep breath, holding it for several seconds, and then releasing it over several more seconds. He should repeat this several times, until he can feel himself calming down.

During this difficult time, you need to control your own anger. You will be mad at what happened that caused your child to become angry (that missed six-inch putt). You will also be angry with your child for his tantrum. Don't join in. It won't be easy, but you will need to console him and help him see what is happening, and perhaps do the breathe – release method together. Remind him that golf is just a game, and let him know that he hasn't let you down. Everyone hits bad shots and misses easy putts.

When your child makes a mistake, he or she needs to "flush" it away and move on. This process is called a mistake ritual, and it is something that can be private between you and your player. The mistake ritual can be a sign or an action that you both recognize, such as brushing your hands on your clothing as though you were brushing away the mistake. It could also be making a "flushing" motion as though the mistake was being flushed down the toilet. The ritual itself is unimportant, but its use is paramount.

When he was younger, my son and I developed a plan that worked, at least sometimes. We sang a silly song from one of his favorite Lightening McQueen videos. The scene is from one of the shorts called "Mater's Tall Tales," where Mater the tow truck dreams of being a rock star. Mater sings a song where the only lyrics are the word "dadgum," over and over.

When Alex hit a poor shot, we looked at each other and sang the "dadgum" song. Now that he is older, we brush it away and move on to the next shot, with a new plan aimed at recovery.

It isn't the end of the world… it is only one bad shot; maybe one penalty shot. Many times it is still possible to make a great par save, or at least save bogey. Then we can go to the next tee feeling like we succeeded, and tee off with a positive attitude. The important thing is to put the bad shot in the past; nothing will change it. The only thing you and your player can do is go forward with your best effort on the next shot. Singing "dadgum" or brushing it away works for us. If this approach works for you, great. If not, find a mistake ritual that you and your player can use as a trigger to recognize what is happening and get back on track as quickly as possible.

Sometimes, even a great mistake ritual doesn't get the job done, and your player struggles to put the error in the past. In those cases, tell your player that a bad shot is like a heavy weight. When he is complaining about a mistake, it is like carrying that heavy weight around. There is no way to hit the next shot with that heavy weight on his shoulders, so he needs to drop it and move on.

I think the best players see mistakes as opportunities to make incredible recoveries. Mistakes provide challenges to be met or chances to show off their short game skills. Indeed, mistakes and imperfect shots add spice and interest to what would otherwise be a very boring game!

The truth is that all golfers, from the greatest to the beginner, hit imperfect shots. Bad shots are to be expected. And, since we expect them to happen, we shouldn't get mad because they do. With something as difficult as golf, we know there are going to be plenty of bad shots, so help your player embrace mistakes and enjoy the opportunities they provide.

Time Management and Focus

One of the greatest challenges of golf is time management. A typical 18-hole round will take about five hours, during which your player will spend less than three minutes actually hitting his or her golf ball. If you count the time taken to prepare for each stroke, your player will spend only 90 minutes or less thinking about hitting the ball. That leaves three and one-half hours of time doing "other stuff," like walking to the ball, talking to fellow-competitors, and the inevitable goofing around.

Golfers need to be able to focus when required and relax the remainder of the time. This ability to "turn on" and "turn off" requires considerable skill, maturity, and an "on-off" switch.

Golfers also need to "stay in the moment." That means to focus on what is happening now. There is no point dwelling on the past, since it cannot be changed. And it can be even worse to think of the future and all of the wonderful things that will happen if this next putt goes in. I call this "getting out of your time zone." When you get out of your time zone, the present will step right up and pull you back in. Violently.

As you undoubtedly know, there is a time for relaxing and a time for focusing. The challenge is doing each at the right time and being able to switch between being "on" and "off." The following timeline illustrates the lifecycle of a golf shot:

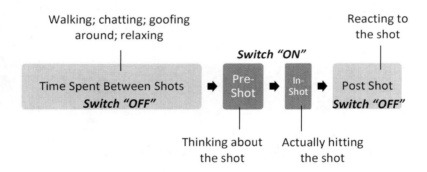

The Value of a Pre-Shot Routine

A pre-shot routine is the stuff your child does right before he or she hits the ball, and it is one of the best ways for your player to stay in his time zone. If you really think about it, he already has a pre-shot routine, since he does *something* before swinging. However, unless he does the same thing every time, and unless it has a purpose, his current pre-shot routine needs to be upgraded. If his coach hasn't worked on it with him, you need to do it, because his pre-shot routine is the key to flipping the "on" switch, getting in the moment, blocking out distractions, and focusing on the only thing that matters: the next shot.

The pre-shot routine is the place where all of the distractions can be put aside and your player can begin to really focus on the task at hand. The switch is flipped to "on" and your player gets down to the business of hitting the next shot. There are three basic things that must be included in his or her pre-shot routine:

1. **Think** – Now is the time for your player to think about what he or she intends to do. What is needed for this shot? How far must it carry? What shot shape is best? What external factors are present (such as wind, cold, uphill, downhill, sidehill, etc.) that may affect the shot? What kind of lie does the ball have (sitting up nicely, down in the grass, against the grain of the grass, wet grass, hardpan, etc.). What club is needed to accomplish the shot? There may be others, but these are the basic things that need to be considered.

2. **Feel** – How does your player want to feel both before and after hitting the shot? The point of this is to imagine hitting a good shot and feeling good about what happened. Golf is a highly mental game, and the pre-shot routine is the place to feel good about things, such as being ready to make a good swing, feeling good about the club and the type of shot that has been selected, recalling good memories of prior

shots in similar situations or with the same club, and knowing that you have done your best.

3. **Act** – The pre-shot routine gives us our last chance to rehearse the exact swing that we intend to use for the upcoming shot. I'll discuss the topic of practice swings more in a bit, but suffice it to say that now is the time for a final rehearsal before "going on stage" and hitting the ball. This process should instill good muscle memories and reinforce the physical swing feeling needed for the shot. The rehearsal doesn't have to be a "practice swing." It can be any swing movement that ingrains the desired muscle memory.

All great players use a pre-shot routine. Although those routines share many similarities, they are unique to each player based on their temperament and needs. We all have different internal clocks and swing tempos to match. Our thought processes differ as we concentrate on hitting the ball. Your child's pre-shot routine should match his style and rhythm, and include the items that help him focus on making his best effort on each shot. Even though they differ, the best pre-shot routines share some common characteristics:

– They are customized to the unique needs of each player.

– They are consistent, always including the same physical movements and thoughts. For example, most pre-shot routines include focusing on the target, gripping the club, aligning the body, and waggling or other methods to keep loose over the ball before swinging.

— They are brief, lasting only around 10 seconds, and do not add significant time to the "shot clock." Generally, your player must hit his shot within 45 seconds, once it is his turn to play. Keep his pre-shot routine brief and do as much shot preparation as possible while others are playing their shots.

— They are used for every shot, and even re-used if something interrupts the pre-shot routine before the swing begins. When interruptions occur, the best players step away and start over from the beginning of the pre-shot routine.

You know your child and his game better than anyone. Discuss the topic and develop a pre-shot routine that fits his or her personality. If you need more detailed example, here is a recommendation to consider:

— Begin behind the ball, standing directly on an imaginary line that runs through the ball to the target. Keep in mind that the target may not be the hole.

— Focus on the target. When doing this, select the smallest possible target. It isn't good enough to aim at the fairway, the green, or even at a house in the distance. Aim at a marker, or perhaps a rake next to a bunker, or at a window on that house. I'm not saying that your child is good enough to control his ball that precisely. I am saying that when he focuses on a small target, his concentration improves and he will have a better chance of being close to his target.

— Breathe. Exhale.

— Take what I call a rehearsal swing while still standing on the target line. This is not a "practice" swing, but a rehearsal swing where he envisions the kind of shot he will make and rehearses the swing that will produce that shot. I recommend only one rehearsal swing, but two is okay. Not three.

— Imagine the ball flying along the target line and hitting the bulls-eye. Great golfers say they actually see a movie in their heads, with the ball traveling exactly as they planned. He should think about what he *wants* to happen, not about what he doesn't want.

> **"Don't think about an elephant (bet you just did!)"**
> **Bill Bozenhart, PGA**
>
> **"Always supply your brain with a positive swing thought. What you think about might just happen."**

— Walk up to the ball, aim the clubface, take his stance, look at the target one last time, and swing.

This exact pre-shot routine may not work for your child, so customize it as needed. Most importantly, make sure he does it on every shot. It will help to forget about the first tee jitters, about the out-of-bounds lurking to the right, about the water in front of the green, and about needing a par to shoot a personal best score.

Of course, there are many other aspects of managing your player's mental game. Just like you and I, he gets nervous on the first tee. He also gets nervous trying to finish his round, especially if he is playing well.

The Fallacy of Practice Swings

The pre-shot routine topic often brings up the subject of "practice swings." Quite candidly, I am not a big fan of practice swings, and I generally recommend that your child not do them. I find that repeated swings frequently serve a *negative* purpose, and they also can be a major cause of slow play. How can something that is supposed to be a positive reinforcement turn into a negative one? It is all in the mind.

When we are preparing to hit our ball, we want to be full of confidence that we can make our best swing and hit the shot we envision. However, many golfers lack that confidence and take repeated practice swings in an attempt to groove the swing right before putting it into action. Unfortunately, there are two common outcomes from practice swings, and neither one leaves the player feeling confident.

If the player makes what feels like a perfect practice swing, his next thought is frequently something like "Uh-oh, I just wasted my one good swing. I'll never do it again." Thus, the perfect practice swing can leave the player with doubt as he prepares to hit his ball.

On the other hand, if the player makes poor practice swings and can't seem to get the right feeling, he may think

"Oh no, I can't seem to get this right. I hope I don't swing this way at the ball." Once again he is filled with doubt and anxiety as he prepares for the shot.

The last time I checked, doubt and anxiety were two things a person would definitely *not* like to have while preparing to hit a golf ball 100 yards over water. Or off the first tee in front of a crowd. Or while standing over a three footer to finish a great round. It is one thing to get loose and swing the club freely while focusing on the target. It is quite another to fall into a "practice swing rut" over the ball.

For this reason, I favor making what I call a "rehearsal swing." Most golfers are constantly working on their swings, trying to incorporate a new swing thought or something from last Saturday's lesson. It is better to rehearse portions of the swing, thinking about a swing drill, and not actually making a real golf swing. For example, if a player is working on improving his rotation, he might benefit from swinging at an imaginary ball that is waist-high, emphasizing rotation rather than lateral shifting. Rehearsal swings can be very effective reminders in a pre-shot routine, and they produce a positive feeling, rather than a "don't do this" swing thought.

When it comes to pitching, chipping or putting, your player should rehearse the speed or force to be applied to the ball, in an effort to feel the proper stroke for distance control. Many junior golfers will approach a chip or putt and take wild practice swings that do nothing to build the correct muscle memory for the actual stroke. Instead, rehearsing for speed should be a part of their short game pre-shot routine.

As an example, when putting, your player should use his regular pre-shot routine as he lines up the putt and figures the break. Then, when next to the ball, he should rehearse the speed, thinking of having the ball stop only about one foot past the hole. In chapter 6 (Making Practice Fun), I have some suggestions for working on putting distance control, which is the number one challenge for most young golfers.

In the meantime, encourage your player to make rehearsal swings for distance control on all short game shots, including putting, chipping, pitching, and bunker shots. When he asks you whether a particular swing "looks right," tell him to use his best judgment. There is no way for you to be sure how much force he intends to apply to the ball, and arguments over your answer are sure to ensue when he leaves it short or rams it by ("you said that was how hard to swing, dad"). Speed control is the player's responsibility, and he needs to make that decision on his own.

The Post-Shot Routine

You may not have thought about having a post-shot routine, but I think it is extremely important. A good post-shot routine can be the thing that helps your player accept what just happened and move on to the next shot in a positive frame of mind. A good post-shot routine can even work like a "time warp" and help make the shot itself better.

In the pre-shot routine, your player needed to turn the switch "on" and accomplish three things: think, feel, and act. Now, he or she needs to undo these as a way to turn the switch "off" and get back to the more relaxing between-shot mode. Therefore, we will do these in reverse order:

1. **Act** – Now is the time to look like a pro and hold that "tour pose" finish. So what if it wasn't a great

shot? Your player can still look professional. Here is how the "time warp" works: if he commits to achieving a tour pose finish no matter what happens to the ball, some sort of magic seems to take place. Your player's finish is a reflection of what led up to it; that is, the swing itself. It is actually somewhat difficult to make a horrible swing and have a beautiful, balanced tour pose finish. Conversely, it is similarly difficult to have a beautiful, balanced swing and have a miserable finish. My experience has shown that the simple objective of finishing with a balanced tour pose will cause the swing to be balanced, and will help improve the shot itself.

2. **Feel** – This is the hard part, especially for young golfers. In order to act and look like a pro, your player needs to be detached from the result of the shot. Detachment means acceptance of what happened. It doesn't mean indifference, or not caring, or quitting. Detachment means "it is what it is," good or bad. Your player doesn't have to like a bad shot, or even to understand why it happened. It just did. He needs only to accept that it wasn't what was expected, and that it isn't the end of the world. It can't be "fixed" on the course (that is why we practice). The shot is done and gone and cannot be taken back. It must be accepted and your player must move on to the next shot.

3. **Think** – The final step to turning the switch "off" is to re-assess the strategy for the remainder of the hole based on this latest shot. Perhaps the shot came off

as intended, and your player's strategy for the hole is intact. Perhaps not. The best way to move on from here is to simply recognize that golf is a fluid game, and your player's strategy needs to be flexible. Maybe it was a birdie hole when the ball was back on the tee, but now a bogey would be a great score. Your player should develop a flexible mentality that sees each subsequent shot as a new beginning to the remainder of the hole, complete with new challenges to recover or attack and make the best of whatever situation arises.

Surely, when people say that golf teaches life lessons, they are thinking of the post-shot routine!

A Matter of Control

So much of the mental game of golf comes down to control, or lack thereof. We think we should be able to control our golf ball and make it behave the way we want it to, but our ball seems to have other ideas. The mental game is a very mature topic, and is an extremely difficult one for young golfers to master. Try to give your player some leeway and try to understand that he or she just simply may not be able to control all of his or her emotions.

I recommend that you and your player have a casual discussion, away from the golf course. The subject of this conversation? Control.

Everything that happens in your player's golf world can be divided into two groups: things that cannot be controlled, and things that can. There are many things that cannot be controlled. These include:

- The weather
- Other players
- Where the ball ends up
- What kind of lie the ball has
- Winning
- Competition
- Golf course conditions
- What happened on the prior hole
- What happened on the prior shot
- What happened one second ago
- The future

Fortunately, there are also quite a few things that your player *can* control. These include:

- His attitude
- What he does before hitting the ball
- What he does when hitting the ball
- What he does after hitting the ball
- Emotions and feelings
- What he pays attention to
- His level of focus
- Staying in the present

The point of this discussion is to have a frank conversation about what he or she can and cannot control. What can your player do about those things that cannot be controlled? Nothing. They must be accepted as-is, because they cannot be changed. I advise my students to love these things. Why do anything else? As hard as they may try, those things cannot be controlled. Your player should not let those things control him or her. They must simply be accepted as facts of life.

And, what should we do with those things that can be controlled? Well... we should control them! Change them as needed to suit our needs or to help us in any way possible. That is how we can make the most of our golf game (and our life), and that is how to survive the mental challenges of golf.

•   •   •

Even though it requires great physical skill, motor control, and coordination, golf is largely a mental game. Managing that game is crucial to maximizing your child's performance on the golf course. Bobby Jones said that "competitive golf is played mainly on a five and one-half inch course... the space between your ears."

Perhaps no place demonstrates this better than a PGA Tour event. Watching the pros warm up hitting balls at the driving range before teeing off, you might think they would all shoot a 65. However, only a few will go that low, and many will come in over par. Their swings are solid, as evidenced by their ball striking on the range, but their scores may vary by 15 strokes or more. The difference is mental — how they utilize their talents and how they manage their way around the course.

Your child is far too young to have the wisdom and maturity required to manage his emotions and think clearly in the face of pressure and adversity. Your overriding job as his coach and caddy is to help him through the character-building moments that golf is guaranteed to supply, and be his emotional crutch so that he can perform to the best of his abilities. He will never admit it, but he needs you for this role more than anything.

In the process, you will probably take more abuse and have more venomous words hurled at you than any person should ever have to endure. Let them slide off your back and allow your child to vent his anger and frustration. At his young age, he isn't as skilled as we are at cursing, throwing clubs, yelling, and slamming clubs into bags. At least I hope not! You are his focal point and his only outlet. Take one for the team and move on to the next shot. There will be time after the round to discuss the situation and how each of you performed according to your respective player and caddy job descriptions as outlined in chapter 1.

CHAPTER FOUR

"You cannot teach greatness. You can only shine the light on the greatness already within."
— TERRI STEC

Starting Your Child in Golf

Many parents want to introduce their children to golf at an early age, and many kids enjoy swinging a stick at a ball as soon as they learn to walk. Our son was one of them, and I found myself wondering how to apply my PGA teaching experience to this new challenge. How do you teach golf to such a young child? By now, I'm sure you know that my perspective on golf for kids is to keep it fun!

But there is another angle that is of paramount importance as you introduce your child to golf: make it easy. In reality, this advice applies to anyone trying to learn this difficult game. If you are a golfer, you know how hard it is to make a golf ball behave. For children who don't yet have the motor control skills and the finesse, balance and coordination, golf can be too frustrating. Your attempts to get your toddler to hit a ball could end in disappointment, and he may not want to come back for more.

Other sports can be difficult as well, but they have introduced ways to make them friendlier. Bowling alleys have bumpers, or guard rails, to keep the ball out of the gutter. How much fun would it be to go bowling if every ball was a gutter ball, and you never knocked down a single pin?

Tennis has QuickStart, which uses larger and less lively balls, a smaller court, and a much lower net. How much fun would it be if you played tennis on a court the size of a basketball court while hitting over a net that was as high as you were tall? Kids love bowling, and tennis is growing in popularity due largely to these efforts.

Golf hasn't yet gotten there. Golf clubs are big and heavy, the hole is too small, courses are too long, and the ball is too hard to hit. If you want your child's first experiences with golf to be fun and inviting, and if you want him to come back for more, you need to make it fun and easy.

Learning Golf

The process of teaching golf to children requires a great deal of patience and a tolerance for their mistakes. This can be a tough task for anyone, and it is even harder for parents because we have a vested interest in the outcome,

> How quickly our children learn to play video games! I wonder how well it would go if we were looking over their shoulders, directing every move, criticizing every mistake, and making them feel like a failure.

and we want our children to learn rapidly. It can be extremely difficult to watch mistakes and wait for the trial and error process to lead to improvement. However, that is how the learning process works.

If you are like most of us and your child has a hand-held game device, consider how he learned to play a video game. At first, he couldn't figure out how to navigate the maze or to land the F-18 on the aircraft carrier. The next day, he is a pro at it. His newfound expertise came from the motivation (fun) to make hundreds of attempts, many of which failed.

No one was there to criticize his technique or methods. No one was shouting directions or telling him what to do and how to do it. He figured it out by himself, and he owned the process. That, in many ways, is how golf should be learned; it just takes longer because of the physical skills involved.

My message is this: when introducing your child to golf, keep it fun and easy, and keep out of the way except for safety or other concerns. It's okay if he putts the ball off the green, or takes ten strokes to get the ball in the hole from three feet away. Let him watch you doing it and challenge him to be a "copycat." Even if you are not a good golfer, you can still model the correct behavior and form. At least you will be better than your child (for now anyway), and he can look up to you as a role model. Soon enough, if he is interested, you can seek the assistance of a PGA/LPGA teaching professional.

Equipment

I recommend starting your child with right-sized clubs and a big beach ball. By "right-sized" clubs, I mean clubs that are the right length and weight. I grew up using cut-down adult clubs, because junior clubs were not available. Now there are several options from companies including U.S. Kids Golf, Nike, Taylor Made, Callaway, and others.

U.S. Kids Golf has the most variety for sizing and playability, including Ultralight clubs for beginners and Tour Series clubs for more serious players, with 9 different lengths available in 3" increments beginning at 39" (for kids 39" tall). With those options, U.S. Kids has right-sized clubs for nearly every junior golfer. Moreover, the U.S. Kids Tour Series clubs are far and away the best quality golf clubs for more serious golfers (I am not affiliated with U.S. Kids Golf, Inc.). Although I have experimented with many "play" clubs for toddlers, I have yet to find one that is safe, soft, and durable. If your toddler wants to swing away, you can use any inexpensive plastic club at first.

Once he has a properly sized club, let him go into the back yard and hammer that beach ball all over the place! It makes a great loud sound when hit, it flies around, and it is almost impossible to miss. And that is critical. Your child needs to be successful. It is no fun flailing about at a tiny golf ball and missing it most of the time. When the time is right, use a smaller (6") beach ball… then a tennis ball… then a 2" foam ball… and finally, a golf ball or golf whiffle ball. Instead of a hole, use a hula hoop, laundry basket, plastic swimming pool, or other fun object as a target.

Golf Form

Of course, it is important to do all of this with some semblance of proper form and fundamentals. This is not a golf instruction book, and your local PGA/LPGA teaching professional can give you some excellent advice. However, I don't mind covering what I think is and isn't important as your child discovers his own golf swing.

First, while the fundamentals of grip, stance, and posture are important, they are not as important as balance in the beginning stages, especially for children younger than five years old. Yes, they do need to stand with their feet about shoulder width apart, but don't bother measuring. It is much more important that their feet stay still during their swing, and that they turn and "point the right toe" (left toe for lefties) on their follow-through. And when it comes to the grip, I have a lot of tolerance (at least initially) for variations.

Even right-sized clubs can be too heavy for young muscles, and swinging a heavy club can dramatically affect the form of a golf swing. Imagine yourself trying to swing a sledgehammer. You couldn't do it with a normal golf grip. Your hands would need to be apart to supply the necessary leverage to lift the heavy weight. If your hands were together, your backswing would be flat, or low to the ground, rather than more upright. Once you got to the top of your backswing, it would be very hard to stop your swing and begin a downswing.

That is why many children begin by holding a golf club with their hands apart, and why they find it difficult to avoid over swinging. It took me a year to finally convince my son to slide his hands together. He even had a legitimate 85 yard hole-in-one while swinging his driver with his hands two inches apart! He was four and one-half years old, and then (as now), he "knew" much more than I about how to swing a club. Thankfully, he didn't heed my advice to stick his hands together.

That "let me do it my way" attitude is responsible for many arguments and much frustration when parents try to teach their children to swing a golf club. My advice is that as long as his feet are steady, his hands are on the club in the correct order (left hand on top for right-handed golfers), and he is hitting the ball, let him have some leeway and have fun. He will be more receptive to instruction, and he might even ask for help when he becomes frustrated because, more than anything, he wants to succeed. It is easy to over-coach, so let him explore a bit on his own, and where possible, let him observe other children and adults who are more experienced.

While he is young and enjoying smacking a ball around, give him some fun challenges. I started in our front yard, which has a high hedge between our property and the neighbor's. It was a great challenge and lots of fun for my son to hit balls over the hedge, and he quickly learned how to make his ball go up and over and into the neighbor's yard.

His form wasn't perfect, but he learned rapidly – so rapidly that we had to abandon our yard and move to the driving range for fear of damaging our neighbor's car or house. Now that I think about it, perhaps that is why he loves a practice game we call "timber" (see chapter 6 for an explanation of "timber"). At three years old it was the hedge; at age seven it was pine trees.

Once again, the main point here is to be creative, allow your child to explore and learn on his own, and always to keep it fun. As soon as you move in to adjust his hands on the club, or to reposition his feet, his natural resistance will start and he will tell you to back off. Let him have freedom, but do explore some introductory lessons or classes with your PGA/LPGA professional.

If your child is an older beginner some of the above is not applicable, but the emphasis on self exploration and fun remains. I usually recommend that children age 5 and up begin with a few private lessons and then join a small group class. The private lessons help them get acclimated and start with proper fundamentals, so that when they join the group they don't feel out of place.

With juniors, as with adults, the social aspects of golf are likely to be more important to them than the golf itself. My son loves to attend our golf camps and after school classes… mostly so he can hang out with his friends. Like the other younger ones, he idolizes the older kids and loves challenging them to putting and short game contests. If it means that he is practicing his short game, I'm all for it.

Junior Golf Tournaments

When your child gets more serious about golf and has progressed into a real golfer, it is time to think about junior tournaments and implementing a player development program like the one described in the following chapter. By "real golfer," I mean he can play nine holes from age-appropriate tees following USGA rules, use proper etiquette, and post a score in the 50s or lower.

There are many tournament opportunities for junior golfers. Leading the way again is the U.S. Kids Golf company, which uses local tour operators to conduct hundreds of junior tournaments for kids age 5-14 across the United States and abroad. Check their website at www.uskidsgolf.com for local tour sites near you. Local tours lead to larger and more prestigious state championships and regional events and to the annual world championships, held in Pinehurst, NC. In addition to U.S. Kids Golf, there are also many other local and regional organizations that operate junior golf tournaments. If your child has the motivation, these tournaments are a great way to start.

To some, the idea of playing in tournaments at the tender age of five years old may seem ridiculous or even inappropriate. However, tournaments provide a way to assess your child's progress, and your own as well. And therein are additional sources of frustration as well as the confidence that comes from success. Tournaments played according to USGA rules and on golf courses with age-appropriate tees result in a stark quantification of your child's golf abilities: his score. If your child is doing well and is capable of posting competitive scores and contending to win, you can celebrate with him, keep things positive, and look forward to more competitive opportunities.

On the other hand, if your child is struggling to shoot competitive scores it is easy for you both to become discouraged. I have found there are generally two categories of golfers who are in this group.

First there are those who have not yet achieved the strength, coordination, and ball control skills necessary to be *able* to shoot a low score from their age-appropriate tees. Junior golfers in this category simply cannot shoot a low score because they don't hit the ball far enough and don't have many scoring opportunities.

Even golfers who have had success but who have recently moved up an age division and thus back to longer tees may

> **Success does not have to mean winning.**

find themselves in this category if their skills haven't kept up with their birthdays. If your child is in this category, you can still help him experience success by emphasizing the fun factor, the experience of being there, and focusing on short game goals like chipping and putting.

He can succeed by chipping better than his last round, by putting as well as the other competitors, by avoiding 3-putts, by being a great teammate with you, by hitting an especially long drive, or in so many other ways. It is up to you as coach, caddy, and parent to find ways to help him enjoy playing golf and finding something – anything – to celebrate. For this golfer, it isn't about the score. It's about the process, and it is important to persevere and look for slow and steady progress.

The second category of golfer includes those who have the ability but who haven't yet put the puzzle pieces of their golf game together. They can hit the ball as far as the better players, they have the short game skills, and they have intense motivation. Most or all of the pieces are there, but one or more key parts are either missing or inconsistent. This golfer may shoot scores similar to those of golfers in the first category above, but his potential is greater, and he may be on the cusp of a breakthrough to lower scores. Because of his greater potential, he may more easily become frustrated or discouraged, and you may too.

Here again it is important to find successes to celebrate. He can succeed by using his pre-shot routine, by saving par or bogey, by avoiding big numbers, by sticking to his game plan, by playing a subset of holes as well as the better players, by avoiding 3-putts, by being a great teammate with you, and as above, in so many other ways. Success breeds success, and that breakthrough will come in time. And when it does, your frustration and doubts will melt away, instantly replaced by new goals and challenges to contend and win.

Regardless of which category your child may be in, remember that he is trying his best, that golf is really difficult, and that he really wants to please you. Find a way for that to happen and enjoy the experience of tackling such a challenging game with your child as your partner and teammate.

• • •

Starting your child in golf is an exciting, rewarding, and frequently frustrating experience. If you remember how difficult golf can be and remain patient, the process can be fun and your child will enjoy going to the golf course with you. There were times when my son wanted to go to the driving range, and he would hit literally hundreds of balls. There were other times when he wanted to go to the range, but when we got there he hit one or two balls and then wanted to leave.

I always tried to remember that it was not about me... it was supposed to be about him. So, if he wanted to hit balls for an hour, I let him. If he wanted to go home, we left. No pressure. No consequences. I realize that this may be difficult to do when you have devoted your time and seven dollars for a basket of range balls. However, think of it like a day at the park, with a $7 basket of chicken fingers that he just "had to have," but then only eats one. Enjoy the park. Enjoy the chicken finger. You can't force him to eat the rest, and you can't force him to hit a whole basket of range balls if he doesn't want to. Keep it positive and keep him coming back again and again.

When it is time to go out on the course with your child, make sure he plays from age-appropriate yardages. Even if there are no U.S. Kids/PGA Family Tees marked on your course, you can use the following chart as a guide in determining where he should start each hole. This setup is designed to allow kids to play golf the way courses are designed – reaching greens in regulation and having chances for pars and birdies.

U.S. Kids / PGA Family Course Yardage Model

Boys	Girls	Holes Played	U.S. Kids Tee Color	Total Yardage	Typical Yardage Per Hole		
					Par 3	Par 4	Par 5
6 & Under	7 & Under	9	Green	1,100	70	120	200
7	8-9	9	Blue	1,500	90	170	250
8-9	10-11	9	Yellow	1,900	110	220	300
10	12-14	9	Red	2,500	120	300	400
11		18	Red	5,000	120	300	400
12		18	White	5,600	140	330	440
13-14		18	Black	6,000	160	350	480

Table 4.1: Suggested golf course setup yardages for kids.
Source: U.S. Kids Golf, Inc., and PGA Family Tees program.

CHAPTER FIVE

*"A teacher helps a person learn specific tasks.
A coach helps a person achieve goals."*

Developing Your Child's Game

As your child's golf manager, you may be juggling the roles of coach, chauffeur, caddy, and parent. Whether or not you have the necessary background in coaching and development, you should be aware of the process in order to maximize your child's potential. In this chapter I discuss my perspective on early specialization in golf, and once your child commits to golf, my concept of a holistic player development program that every serious golfer should follow. By serious, I mean those at any age who either play tournament golf or who want to develop their golf skills to their fullest potential, especially those playing in high school and seeking a college scholarship.

This program is likely to be similar to one you would find in a formal golf academy. Such academies can cost tens of thousands of dollars per year and require total immersion in golf. That may be too much for you in both money and time. Few people have the necessary resources to commit to a peak performance academy. Moreover, full-time golf academies are usually tailored for high school-age golfers, and may not be appropriate for younger children.

Even though your child may be too young (and you may not yet be ready to ship him off to a boarding academy), you can still follow a player development program with some discipline and structure and gain some of the benefits of the academy approach. One of the key attributes of this approach is that it follows a consistent system, rather than randomly working on golf swing mechanics and reacting to problems as so many of us are prone to doing. It is consistent and proactive.

Another attribute of this approach is that the program follows a coaching model, working on all aspects of your child's golf game. A key requirement is to enlist the expertise and guidance of an experienced PGA/LPGA teaching professional who is willing to follow a holistic coaching philosophy. As in medicine, a holistic approach addresses the entire golfer and all aspects of his game. Although this is a more time-intensive approach, it is may be exactly what you are already doing for your child.

After all, you house him, feed him, sign him up for golf classes and golf camps, enter him in tournaments, help him grow stronger, train him, and teach him. You simply need a trained PGA/LPGA professional as a partner to help you coordinate his overall training program.

Finding the right professional might not be easy. Many excellent teachers don't have the time or resources to provide full coaching assistance, and may be limited to teaching periodic lessons.

However, before you leap headfirst into a comprehensive, holistic golf training program, let's step away from the edge and think about the pressing and somewhat controversial topic of early specialization.

Early Specialization

If you haven't already felt it, thought it, or discussed it with your spouse, you will soon. The conversation goes something like this:

"Honey, don't you think _____ (insert your child's name) should quit playing _____ (Insert a sport like baseball, basketball, soccer, football, etc.) and just focus on golf?"

It doesn't matter who initiates the discussion, because we all think it and hear it from others. It happens on the practice range when someone says "he looks like the next Tiger Woods," or "she is going to be the next Annika Sorenstam." There is no doubt that it is an amazing thing to watch a talented youngster hit golf balls like a miniature pro. And, it is easy to believe that he or she will grow into the next Tour superstar. So, we channel them towards golf at the expense of other athletic activities. After all, we don't want our 8-year old's golf swing to be ruined by swinging a baseball bat (trust me... that won't happen!).

However, it can be challenging to involve your young golfer in other sports. Unfortunately, many coaches of other sports demand dedication to their sport, so the issue presents itself sooner than you might think. In spite of the wonderful benefits of multi-sport participation, there is incredible pressure to specialize in a single sport at an early age.

It is understandable that team sport coaches want each player to be a 100% dedicated team member. After all, that is what is best for the team. And, it is understandable that we golf parents want our children to focus on golf and make the most of their talents. However, when viewed from the youth athlete's perspective, early specialization could be the worst approach.

Research and history both show that the greatest athletes were multi-sport athletes when they were young, and they specialized in their chosen sport later; usually in their teens. Multi-sport participation builds speed, strength, hand-eye coordination, and diversity. Multi-sport athletes are more balanced physically, leading to fewer cumulative injuries from overuse or repetitive motions. In addition to becoming well-rounded physically, multi-sport participation can help golfers be more team-oriented and well-rounded mentally. Finally, multi-sport athletes have less chance of burnout, which is a significant concern for young golfers.

As a golf parent, it is easy to fall into the pattern of pushing your young golfer to practice and play golf in every spare moment. We see professional golfers practicing non-stop (it's their job), and we know the hours on the range and on the putting green are needed. Then, when we see or hear about another child who spends every afternoon taking lessons and then plays golf every weekend, we feel as though our child is somehow "falling behind."

I like to think of 14 as the critical age for young golfers. Below that age, they should be playing multiple sports, either in school programs or through leagues. It isn't even necessary that golf be number one, but it is important to continue to play and practice golf through those developmental years.

Once they reach 14, it is time to show more commitment and dedication to golf, if that is their chosen sport (let's hope so!). Even then, other sports still play a role in athletic development, but golf should be number one on their list in order to have a chance at competitive golf in high school and beyond.

When we hear about the greatest golfers, we tend to think they all played nothing but golf from the moment they could walk. However, that is the exception; not the rule. For every Tiger Woods (who famously started hitting balls at age 2) or Michelle Wie (who started at 4), there have been dozens of phenomenal golfers who never touched a golf club until they were 10 years old or older. Moreover, many of the greatest golfers in history were multi-sport athletes before committing to golf. Here are a few notable examples.

The greatest golfer of all time (no, Tiger hasn't caught him yet), Jack Nicklaus started at age 10, and he quickly was recognized as a golf prodigy. Still, he also played basketball and football in high school, all while dominating junior golf throughout Ohio and beyond. He didn't play professionally until he was 22 years old, after conquering the world of amateur golf, and went on to win 18 major championships and 73 PGA Tour events.

Sam Snead is regarded as the greatest all-around golf-athlete, and played football, basketball, baseball, and ran track (he could run the 100-yard dash in 10 seconds). He began playing golf after caddying at age 15 and still holds the record for winning the most PGA Tour events with 82, including seven majors.

Annika Sorenstam was a nationally ranked Swedish junior tennis player, who also played soccer and was a highly competitive skier. She switched to golf at age 12, then grew to become the most successful female golfer in history, winning 10 LPGA major titles, 72 LPGA events 18 international tournaments, and more than $22 million dollars.

There are endless more examples of phenomenal golfers who didn't even play golf when they were kids. The point of this is to continue to keep your child's golf in perspective and keep a long-term view of his or her golf development. Be wary of over-practicing and the potential of burnout. And, let your child be a kid and enjoy any and all sports that may interest him or her. There will be plenty of time later to grind on the practice range.

Teaching vs. Coaching

There is a big difference between teaching and coaching. Many teaching professionals work from a "lesson model," where the student shows up for a lesson, something is taught, and the student goes away to practice (hopefully) until the next lesson. This approach is common and can work well for students with a dedicated work ethic who practice diligently and play frequently between lessons, and who don't require the oversight and management of a coach. It doesn't work well for the golfer who hopes to improve and expects to get there by weekly lessons alone.

In his excellent book "Easier Said Than Done," Dr. Rick Jensen describes "the undeniable, tour-tested truths you must know (and apply) to finally play to your potential on the golf course." His book is a sobering indictment of the traditional golf teaching method and describes 12 "truths" that, if followed, will transform anyone's golf game. The coaching model, in tandem with a dedicated and motivated student, can set the stage for significant and lasting improvement.

The coaching model incorporates the traditional lesson teaching model but goes far beyond and organizes all of the areas surrounding your child's golf development in a way that maximizes his or her performance. A true coach is a blend of teaching professional, trainer and mentor. A coach provides the expert swing advice, coordinates interaction with other professionals and specialists, and oversees all aspects of your child's development, including practice, playing, and competition.

If your teaching professional follows the lesson teaching model, your child may need more guidance. Either you can provide the coaching overlay, or you can seek out a professional who is willing to take a more holistic approach. Remember, a coach should focus on total player development. A coach helps identify the skills and capabilities that are within your child. A coach works with your child's existing capabilities and maximizes his performance to the best of his ability. A coach helps your child eliminate weaknesses and improve. A coach helps your child achieve goals.

Teaching Children

Your child's coach should also specialize in teaching children. Many proven teaching techniques that work quite well with adults fail miserably when applied to kids. And, some "regular" teaching practices need to be modified to be more effective with children. For example, an adult may be willing to stand on the range and hit dozens of shots with one club, working on a specific technical drill or exercise. Kids won't do this. To paraphrase Cyndi Lauper, "kids just wanna have fun."

We make junior classes fun at the Don Law Golf Academy by using skill-based educational games that are fun to play and which build golf skills. I'll cover more of this topic in chapter 6, but it is critical that your child's teacher inject fun and games into each lesson.

Adults deal with each other at eye level. Your child's pro should teach at eye level – I do, and I quickly wear out the knees of my golf pants. It is important to communicate directly eye-to-eye and not intimidate the child just by sheer size difference. Check references and observe your teaching professional, and make sure he or she and your child have a good rapport and that lessons are fun and productive.

Player Development Program

Behind all of the emphasis on fun there should be a method that works toward continuous improvement in your child's scores. I have developed a player development program that is structured around the coaching model and addresses each development area, continually refining and improving and honing your child's game as he or she grows and matures. This is a total golf development program that cycles through an ongoing process of performance improvement, repetitively working on each facet of the game. I like to think that the program helps make the most of your child's golf game while revealing and focusing on opportunities for improvement. The program features the following components:

–   **Game Assessment**, where your child's strengths and weaknesses are identified through skills tests;

–   **Skills Improvement**, where your child will focus on the highest priority skills and improvement opportunities with the goal of eliminating or minimizing weaknesses;

- **Player Development**, which addresses how your child can make the most of his current game, including ball control, decision-making, and self management;

- **Swing Mechanics**, where your child will work on technical swing improvements;

- **Knowledge**, which focuses on developing golf knowledge, including golf physics, swing theory, rules, and history of the game; and

- **Fitness and Nutrition**, which focuses on strengthening the mind and body for golf performance.

Again, this is a continuous improvement process that cycles through each of these areas, each time digging deeper and revealing more information about your child's golf game and the steps required to develop peak performance. Figure 5.1 illustrates the program and shows how it cycles continuously through each area. A detailed description of each area of the program follows the diagram.

Figure 5.1: A peak golf performance development cycle.

Game Assessment

The player development program cycle begins with game assessment. At the beginning and repeating on a regular basis, you should identify strengths and weaknesses in each aspect of your child's game through performance measurement and analysis. This assessment will form the basis of an improvement plan that will be addressed in other areas of the cycle.

Performance measurement can be done in many ways, but the essence is to conduct a skills test that covers all key areas of golf performance, including driving, approach shots, all short game areas, putting, and ball control. Appendix 1 shows sample skills test forms that can be used for this purpose.

However, before discussing your child's specific game assessment, let's take a look at the components of a golf score. Each round of golf includes these areas:

- Driving (tee shots)
- Fairway or Rough Shots (woods or long irons)
- Approach Shots (from 20 or more yards)
- Pitching (from 3-20 yards off the green)
- Bunker Shots
- Chipping (from the fringe of the green)
- Putting

How do these areas contribute to a total score? Which ones are most important? Which ones are strengths and which are weaknesses for your child? To keep things in perspective, consider the following chart:

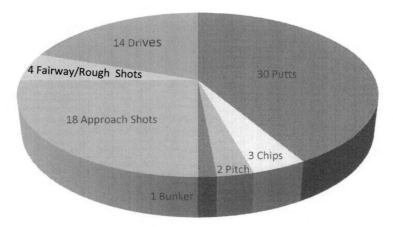

Figure 5.2: The makeup of an even-par round of 72.

Figure 5.2 shows how these seven areas combine in a typical round of golf for a good player who shoots an even-par 72. Notice the *relative importance* or the size of each area; that is, the areas where the most strokes are taken.

Now, let's take a look at the same type of chart for a golfer who shoots a score of 90:

Figure 5.3: The makeup of a score of 90.

The 90-shooter still hits 14 tee shots, because the other 4 holes are par 3s. He still hits 18 approach shots, since there are still 18 holes. He hits two more fairway shots than our par-shooter since he doesn't hit the ball as far and probably cannot reach some par 4 holes in 2 shots. The big difference appears to be in putting and the short game. But why? Are his putting skills deficient? Is his short game weak? Which area is having the greatest impact on his scores?

The challenge in the assessment process is to determine where the most improvement in score can be made; i.e., which area needs the most attention. A significant difference between the 90 shooter and the par shooter is the number of putts, so it is logical to work on putting. The rest of the 90 shooter's short game also probably needs work. Together, putting and short game account for 16 of the 18 shot difference between 72 and 90.

However, what if his approach shots are to blame? Perhaps he takes more putts because his ball is usually far from the hole on those occasions when he finds the green on his approach shots. And, perhaps his short game (chipping, pitching, and bunkers) is getting overworked because he has trouble hitting the green with his approach shots. A game analysis might show that the par shooter hits 12 greens in regulation and the 90 shooter only hits 4 greens in regulation. If his short game is weak, he will still leave long putts to save par or bogey, which again leads to more putts.

Finally, how does his driving contribute to the puzzle? Perhaps his approach shots are poor because they are much longer than approach shots taken by the par shooter, and they are coming from the rough rather than the center of the fairway. Oh yes… and we haven't even considered penalty shots, which are few and far between for the par shooter and which can turn our 90 shooter's score into 100 or more.

The point of all of this is that the game assessment process takes careful thought and, most importantly, data. You should work with your child to collect and maintain detailed performance statistics from actual rounds played (preferably tournament rounds). These stats should include information about driving accuracy, approach shots, short game skills, bunker play, and putting. However, it is easy to overdo things and try to collect too much data, and it isn't easy to remember to write it all down during the round when you are already working hard to count everyone else's scores and keep up with the group in front.

Typical statistics include:

Driving

o   Distance
o   Accuracy (fairways hit)

Greens in Regulation (GIR) – distance of approach shot, whether shot hit green, and distance left to hole for each:

o   Short irons
o   Mid irons
o   Long irons / hybrids

Scrambling Percentage – length of putt remaining after the following, and whether the putt was holed:

o   Chipping
o   Pitching
o   Bunkers

Putting

- o Number of 1-putts, 2-putts, 3-putts, and >3-putts per round
- o Putts per GIR
- o Lagging – distance remaining from long putts
- o Short (3-6 feet) conversion percentage

Penalty Shots, and their cause (e.g., out of bounds, lost ball, unplayable lie, water hazard, and club used that produced the poor shot).

As the caddy, it will be your job to record these stats during the round, or immediately afterward when your memory is fresh. There are handheld apps that assist with this data collection chore, but I find it easier to mark the scorecard and then record the data in a spreadsheet. This is especially important because many tournament rules do not allow the use of handheld devices during play.

Therefore, if you intend to do any computerized analysis, the data need to be entered after the round anyway. The simplest approach is to mark statistics on a golf stats scorecard such as the one included in Appendix 2. Just by making note of your child's game statistics, you will quickly get a good view of his strengths and weaknesses that will feed in to the next stop on the player development cycle.

This data collection and analysis step is also important because it can serve as the proof of where problems lie. Although you may know intuitively what areas of your child's game need work, he may not agree. He needs to understand the message from the data and buy-in to the idea of developing an improvement plan.

The final facet of the game assessment process is to consider your child's knowledge and strategic thinking abilities and how they might contribute to his score. Knowledge in this case refers to his ability to make swing corrections, knowledge of swing mechanics, and understanding of rules and stroke-saving options in trouble situations. Strategic thinking refers to his understanding of his capabilities and limitations, and how best to attack the golf course to make the most of his game.

Skills Improvement

It can be uncomfortable to discuss weaknesses, so let's call them improvement opportunities. Even the best PGA Tour players are not perfect in every area, and they all have opportunities to improve. As the player, your child must willingly analyze his faults, identify those areas where he can improve, and help design a plan to make it happen. We all love to practice what we do well. However, that won't help lower your child's scores.

Once improvement opportunities are identified, a plan should be established focusing on those high-priority skills that present the greatest opportunities for lowering his scores. The analysis should identify the root cause of scoring problems, and the plan should address those areas in priority order. The objective is to achieve consistent shot execution across all areas of your child's game by eliminating or minimizing weaknesses.

I recommend a four-step plan for mastery of each improvement opportunity:

1. **Determine root cause** – When a problem is identified, its cause should be determined. It is quite easy to confuse the symptoms of a problem with the cause of that problem. For example, suppose you determine that your child is taking too many putts per round. I use 15 putts per 9 holes as a standard, or 30 putts per 18 holes. While this might sound low, it would rank only 166th on the PGA Tour in 2014 (the best putter, Justin Leonard, averaged 27.77 putts). Yes, there were 165 other players averaging between 27.77 and 30 putts per 18 holes!

    If putting is a problem, is it due to lack of distance control on long putts, or is it due to inaccuracy with short putts? Or, perhaps his approach shots and short game are to blame because they are leaving too many long, difficult putts. Your statistics should help you find the answer.

2. **Drills and structured practice** – Once the root cause is determined, you or your child's PGA/LPGA professional can recommend practice exercises and drills that will help strengthen his skills. This step includes lots of repetition working through the improvement plan, ideally with expert professional feedback. If professional expertise is not available, your child can use practice games such as those in the ParKit Short Game kit (see chapter 6). For example, if putting distance control is the problem, ParKit's "Lagmaster" game is an excellent and fun way to work on lagging long putts close to the hole.

    Regardless of whether you use fun skill-based games or rote drills, the goal is to build good habits and motor control through repetition and practice. On the other hand, if the remedy is a technical swing issue, it should be addressed in the "swing mechanics" area of the cycle.

3. **Transfer training** – It is one thing to be able to perform a skill in isolated practice, and quite another thing to be able to perform it in competitive conditions, with people watching and your score on the line. Therefore, this step involves exposing the skill to conditions that simulate actual golf competitive conditions, and also using the skill while playing and keeping score. This can be done in practice situations on the range and on the course.

4. **Review, reassess and refine** – The final step is to periodically reevaluate the skill using the same assessment process discussed above. You should record the results and chart his progress as what was once an improvement opportunity becomes a strength.

Player Development

In addition to working on improvement opportunities as identified in the assessment process, your child should work on improving his overall golf scoring abilities using his existing swing mechanics to produce the lowest scores possible. It may seem logical to immediately work on swing mechanics when there is a performance problem. While swing changes may be needed, they are not necessarily going to produce an immediate change. Indeed, swing changes frequently produce a temporary setback while those changes are assimilated into your child's swing. Meanwhile, the show must go on, so in this section your child should work on improving his scoring skills:

- **Ball Control** - In this area, the emphasis is not on swing mechanics or technical details of the swing, but on using his existing swing to control the golf ball in all dimensions.
  - o Directional control
  - o Distance and feel
  - o Trajectory control

- **Decision-Making** – Making the best possible choices to produce the lowest score from whatever situation presents itself throughout the round.
  - o Situation assessment (lie, wind, slope, speed, firmness, sand, etc.)
  - o Strategy
  - o Club selection

- **Self Management** – Controlling your child's emotions (and your own!) and maintaining focus on the shot at hand.
  - o Emotional control
  - o Focus

These are all skills that are integral to lowering your child's scores, and which can be refined regardless of his shot-making abilities or swing technique. Ball control, decision-making, and self management are all critical to making the most of his current abilities. Steady improvement in these areas will help him perform his best, even when his swing fails him and the golf gods toss their lightning bolts at him as they always seem to do.

Golf Swing Mechanics

Here is where your child will work on specific swing mechanical issues and golf swing fundamentals. The objective is to continually refine the swing so that it is trustworthy and repeatable. Swing mechanics are important, but they are often a secondary factor when it comes to scoring. Your child's basic swing mechanics can probably be improved. However, as discussed above, they may not be the primary factors in generating his current scores. His swing should be analyzed and assessed, and he should work on building the most efficient, powerful and repeatable swing possible.

My philosophy is to work with each student's existing swing and enhance it through incremental improvements and changes, rather than making drastic changes or starting from scratch. Millions of words have been written on the golf swing, and this is not a swing instruction book. However, my approach is to focus on these two key areas:

– Efficiency (swing plane, clubface angle, balance)

– Repeatability (tempo, timing, and coordination)

Your child's swing work should include the use of video

analysis, ball flight monitors, and computer swing and ball analysis as needed.

Golf Knowledge

It is easy to get lost in the details of the golf swing and skill development and forget to focus on the bigger picture of the wonderful game of golf itself. Your child needs an appreciation of its history (to them that may include anything that happened before last year) as well as current tour events. You should help develop your child's overall golf knowledge with a focus on rules and golf physics (ball flight laws, swing dynamics, etc.), but also including golf history and reading selections from your local library.

I like to help my students of all ages understand why the golf ball does what it does, and kids are always asking those "why" questions. Here are a few great topics for discussion and my kid-friendly explanations, with full apologies to any physicists, scientists, historians and others who probably know a whole lot more than I about most of this.

–   Why does a golf ball have dimples? Long ago, the first golf balls were leather pouches stuffed with feathers (they were called "featheries"). The feathers were soaked and packed into the pouch, then the pouch was sewed up tight (imagine a baseball) and painted. When it dried, the feathery would fly nicely when smacked with a niblick or mashie. Featheries had stitches and were not perfectly smooth and round, but they were used for nearly 400 years.

When the gutta percha rubber ball was introduced in 1848, it transformed the game. The first gutta percha rubber balls were smooth, but golfers quickly noticed that old used balls would fly better and farther than smooth new ones – the new ones flew more like knuckle balls. It seemed that once they were scraped and dinged from being used, the ball flight improved.

Once this discovery was made, golfers began hammering their golf balls with a sharp pointed hammer to make indentations; these were the first dimpled golf balls. Later on, molds were made with various dimple patterns, which were pressed into new balls.

It turns out that the dimples create turbulence around the ball as it spins backwards (backspin) in flight. This turbulence is similar to that created by an airplane wing. Air pressure builds up under the spinning ball, forcing the ball higher into the air and making it curve predictably right or left, depending on the direction the ball is tilted as it is spinning.

You can conduct your own science experiment by hitting both new and old range balls. If you can find an old ball with a worn surface and minimal dimples, you will see that it seems to float right and left through the air, and that it doesn't stay aloft and carry as far as a new ball with good dimples.

— Why do some clubs have names and some only have numbers? Early golf clubs all had names, like driver, brassie (2-wood), and spoon (4-wood) for what we today call "woods." Irons also had names like cleek

(2-iron), mashie (5-iron), niblick (9-iron), and wedge, plus combinations like mashie niblick (7-iron).

When modern clubs were introduced by Spalding in the early 1930's, the names faded away to be replaced by numbers. However, some names stuck, like "driver" and "wedge."

— Why are clubs called "woods"? Until the late 1980's, which of course seems like the dinosaur age to most junior golfers today, long clubs like the driver were made of hard wood. I grew up playing with a persimmon head driver and laminated 3-wood and 4-wood. I still have the driver, and today I can't imagine how I ever hit it. It is so inferior to today's super-light titanium drivers that it is virtually unplayable, at least to me.

In addition to these topics, there is so much for your child to learn about the history of golf, its characters, golf courses, tournaments, and general trivia. Who today could imagine a PGA Tour professional winning eleven tournaments in a row? Byron Nelson did it in 1945. He went on to win 18 events that year, a record that will never be broken.

Then there is Gene Sarazen, who invented the sand wedge and used his new club to win the 1932 Open Championship. He also hit the "shot heard 'round the world" in the 1935 Masters when he made a double-eagle 2 on the par 5 15th hole at Augusta National, and went on to win the tournament in a playoff.

You could also talk about Ben Hogan, whose work ethic was second to none, and who recovered from a near-fatal car crash in 1949 to win the 1950 US Open and the 1953 Open

Championship at Carnoustie, along with seven other major championships.

Your child probably knows much more about Rickie Fowler or Tiger Woods than he does about Jack Nicklaus, Tom Watson, Arnold Palmer, Gary Player, Sam Snead, Walter Hagen, Bobby Jones, Harry Vardon, Francis Ouimet, or any of the dozens of golfers who dominated their respective eras and made golf what it is today.

When my son met Jack Nicklaus at a local U.S. Kids tournament, he reluctantly agreed to a photo with the Golden Bear. Nicklaus' grandson was playing in the event, and Jack was there as a spectator. Alex had no real idea that Nicklaus was, and still is, regarded as the greatest golfer in history. Will Tiger or anyone ever break his record of 18 major wins? Does anyone remember that Jack also had 19 second place and nine third-place finishes in the majors? Even if Tiger does surpass the 18 major wins, no golfer will ever match Nicklaus' 46 top-3 major finishes.

And does your child know that the winningest PGA or LPGA Tour golfer of all time is Kathy Whitworth, who won 88 LPGA tournaments, six more than Sam Snead? Every child needs a hero to admire and to use as a role model. Do some research together at the computer and learn about these and other legends of golf.

The knowledge stop on the player development cycle also includes improving your child's knowledge of the rules of golf. The rules chapter in this book is only a superficial discussion of the rules of golf. Even though I joke about 34 rules requiring 181 pages to explain them, the USGA Rules of Golf book is good and required reading for your junior golfer. Its extension, called "Decisions on the Rules of Golf," is even more interesting, and describes just about every crazy thing that can happen to a golf ball and what to do about it. I highly recommend buying and reading both books.

Lastly, there are many excellent golf books that cover golf swing theories and practices, instruction, history, physics, and every other topic imaginable. I have listed some of my favorites in Appendix 3. When your child is old enough to appreciate them, these books will make for great conversation pieces, as everyone has their own theories and ideas about how to hit a golf ball.

Fitness and Nutrition

Much has been written lately on the subject of golf fitness and the importance of proper nutrition, especially while playing. If you are able to connect with a Titleist Performance Institute (TPI) certified professional and a personal trainer, you can work with them to develop an overall fitness and health plan designed to put your child in peak condition for golf performance.

If such professionals are unavailable, you can still work on flexibility, strength, and stamina with your child. Just use extreme caution with exercises, especially with young children. Their bodies really don't need fitness equipment or workout regimens.

In fact, one of the best ways to ensure your child develops physically is to encourage him or her to play other sports in addition to golf. Soccer, baseball, and tennis are all excellent sports that help build balance, coordination, flexibility, and strength... all while having fun playing the game.

Once your child is older and ready to think about specializing in golf, golf-specific training can begin. Modern golf development is highly focused on total player development, and there are timelines and schedules that illustrate how young bodies grow and develop. These show how to best facilitate the physical development process, when to train for coordination vs. strength and flexibility, and how to integrate a training plan into your child's golf development.

While the above ideas are long-term development suggestions, you can take immediate action to ensure that your child eats and drinks properly before and during competition. It is difficult enough for your young golfer to maintain focus during a long round of golf, and almost impossible to do so when hungry or thirsty. Keep a water bottle and his favorite healthy snacks handy at all times (one of your daddy caddy duties). We use sliced apples, peanut butter crackers, bananas, and granola bars to keep the energy level up.

•   •   •

Before even thinking about diving into a comprehensive golf development program, your should first think about the early specialization issues. Make sure your child develops as an athlete first, then as a golfer. Elite golfers need their entire body and mind to be strong and in balance, and other sports can help you achieve that goal while keeping your child from overdosing on golf.

Keep in mind that your child's golf development program is a cycle. That means that once an improvement plan is prepared, he will work through each area of the program, refining and improving his game incrementally and returning to the game assessment process again and again. If the process is working, each subsequent assessment should show progress, and his scores should start to drop. Each time through the cycle, each area (e.g. knowledge or fitness) can be revealed in more depth, keeping his or her interest peaked and creating a steady learning and improvement process.

CHAPTER SIX

"The same kid who will perform a practice drill for only 5 minutes will play a fun practice game for 5 hours."

— DON LAW, PGA

Making Practice Fun

A recent study of kids' reactions to various words showed that the word "practice" ranked just below "broccoli" and "homework" on the kid-o-meter (just kidding!). But let's face it. No kid likes to practice, whether it is the piano or golf. They just wanna have fun, remember?

We recognized this years ago at the Don Law Golf Academy and developed many fun, skill-based educational games that we use in our junior golf classes. If you want your child to develop a true love for the game of golf, his or her early golf experiences need to be fun, exciting, and challenging. The golf course should be a fun place for him to be, full of joy and play – almost like going to the playground. And, your child's interactions with you on the golf course should be playful and fun.

I'm not saying that the golf course is a playground; it isn't, and your young golfer needs to behave with appropriate etiquette and respect at the golf course. However, there are plenty of ways to create fun games that require golf skills in order to play them successfully. That is what my colleagues and I did when we created ParKit Golf, Inc. We market those games and associated props to other teaching pros who want to make their junior golf classes and camps more fun, and to parents who want to encourage their golfing children to practice short game skills. With ParKit, we took boring practice drills and turned them into fun games that kids of any age will enjoy playing, without even thinking that they are practicing.

As much as you want your child to practice and improve, he may not share your level of motivation. My experience has shown that if you care more about golf than your child cares about golf, things don't go too smoothly, and the problems first emerge in practice sessions. When our son showed an interest in golf at a very early age, I made a pledge that I have kept to this day. It hasn't been easy! I promised to take him to the golf course whenever he wanted to go. And, I promised to never force him to go to the golf course when he didn't want to go. The latter promise has been the most painful to keep, but I hope it helps preserve his love for the game.

Like many of you, I want my son to take advantage of his God-given talents. I want him to have a practice ethic and a drive to improve. He just wants to have fun. I want him to work on his weaknesses and hit hundreds of shots from 40 yards and in. He just wants to have fun. I want him to stay on the putting green until he can learn how to 2-putt from any-where. He just wants to have fun. I want him to *want* to go to the golf course to practice. Many times, he would rather ride his bike. So we ride bikes, go swimming, play tennis, and do other things instead of practicing, often right before tourna-ments. I take a long-term view. He is doing great right now, and he loves golf. I want him to love golf when he is in his teens, and I'm willing to suppress my desires now so that he doesn't burn out later.

When we do go to practice, we play games. Sometimes it is just him competing against some imaginary world record that he set in a prior practice session. Other times he and I compete head-to-head in areas where short game skills require finesse and touch rather than strength. Frequently he finds a friend at the course and they putt and chip for fun. I try not to worry too much about his technique or the results. It is enough to know that he is there, enjoying himself and spending quality time around the green.

Here are some of the games that work for us. Try incorporating these into your next practice session and emphasize the fun — the way it would be if you and your child went to the park, or bike riding, or to the beach.

On and Around the Putting Green

As I discussed earlier, the number one challenge faced by junior golfers is distance control. They will never miss a 10 foot putt by 6 feet to the right or left. They will, however, routinely slam a 10 foot putt so that it goes 10 feet past the hole! As his ball flies over the top of the hole and rolls to the edge of the green, he will assure you that he "almost made that one." You know better, but it is a losing argument.

For distance control, try playing a game called "Catch Me If You Can"[1]. This fun game is great for putting, chipping, pitching, and even full swings. The object of Catch Me is to hit as many balls in a row as possible where each ball travels farther than the prior ball without going beyond a boundary limit that you set. Each ball must "catch up to" the

---

[1] Catch Me If You Can is copyrighted by ParKit Golf, Inc. Used with permission.

prior ball. The winner is the player who hits the most consecutive shots farther then the prior ball before going out of bounds.

If your child tends to hit putts too far, as most do, try a variation on Catch Me that I call "Sneak Attack." "Sneak Attack" is the inverse of Catch Me, in that the object is to avoid going too far. Begin by putting a ball toward the edge of the green, trying not to go over the edge. Then, putt subsequent balls from the same starting point so that each ball "sneaks up" on the prior ball, but doesn't touch it or go past it. Each successful sneak attack earns a point. See how many times your child can do this, and give him a reward if he can reach 20 points.

For accuracy, try playing a game of "tag" with your putters and golf balls. Like regular tag, one player is "it" and the other player tries to avoid being tagged. The player who is "it" tries to putt his ball so that it touches the other player's ball. Unlike regular tag, players alternate being "it" on each shot. You will find your child really focusing hard on where your ball goes, aiming carefully, and reading the break as he tries to putt his ball into yours. Tag is great fun and it keeps him putting productively for a long time.

Full Swings

Practicing the long game is often fun because almost everyone loves pounding drivers on the range. However, driver tee shots account for only about 15-20% of strokes taken in a round of golf. Most golfers will spend 50% or more of their practice time hitting drivers, and only 20% of their time on the putting green. That is backwards. Yes, it is important to hit long and accurate drives, but it is even more important to hit accurate approach shots to the green. These short and mid-iron shots represent 25% of strokes taken and are critical scoring clubs. The nearer these shots are to the hole, the less pressure your child will feel on his putting game. As with putting, however, these clubs are usually not practiced effectively and sufficiently. This pattern is true for kids as well as adults, so we need to get creative with full swing practice sessions.

One of my son's favorite practice games is "timber," which we invented to have fun hitting short and mid-iron shots. There are large trees around our practice range, and we position ourselves so that he can aim at a tree. He then hits shot after shot with different clubs, trying to hit different parts of the tree. We call it "timber" because, in our imaginations, he is cutting down the tree bit by bit. When a leaf or branch does fall, we yell "timber!" In reality, no harm is done, and he has loads of fun making his ball ricochet left and right off branches, the trunk, dead limbs, and leaves. In the process, he will hit literally hundreds of balls at tiny targets way up high and far away. What great practice!

Again, I try not to worry too much about specific technique unless he is having trouble. It is more important that he is incredibly focused on a very small target, he is controlling his ball's direction and trajectory, and he is laughing to the point of tears after every swing.

I realize that you may not have access to a practice facility that has such conveniently positioned trees, but the concept could apply to almost any range target (especially the range picker). The main point is to get creative and find ways to make practicing more fun.

Seriously Fun Practice

I know what you may be thinking: "All of this fun and games stuff is not for me. I want my kid to work hard and practice until his hands bleed." Well so do I, but I can't tell him that, and I certainly can't make him do it.

The truth is that many parents initially have a negative reaction to having their child play practice games, thinking that they are somehow not serious enough. In reality, however, the above games and many more like them are quite serious. Variations of these games are used by tour players of all caliber. Still, I understand the stigma that may be associated with game playing, and the feeling that it applies only to the youngest players. So here are some suggestions for older juniors and more serious tournament players of any age who may be acquiring a stronger practice work ethic. Even if these are not considered "games," I recommend using your imagination to help make practice more fun. We can all remember imagining a putt to win the Masters when we were kids practicing on the putting green.

How To Practice

Everyone knows the saying attributed to the late great coach Vince Lombardi: "Practice doesn't make perfect. Perfect practice makes perfect." While there may be differences of opinion on exactly what perfect golf practice is, we probably all understand what it isn't. It is not using one ball on the putting green and randomly putting to different holes. It is not chipping one ball from a perfect lie on the fringe with a sand wedge to a hole across the green. It is not standing on the range hitting shot after shot to no specific target. Still, this is how many junior golfers "practice." We adults do it too.

I think there are four basic categories or ways of practicing. Whether or not you choose to incorporate fun and games, your child's practice sessions should follow these guidelines. These four are repetition, variation, simulation, and integration.

Repetition Practice

Whether on the putting green or the tee, golf is about controlling the golf ball. Aside from the mental aspects discussed in chapter 3, ball control is about motor control, and the first aspect of motor control is the ability to repeat a particular movement. Repetition practice involves practicing the same stroke or shot again and again, striving to be able to repeat the outcome.

On the putting green, this might involve hitting dozens of putts from the same starting point to the same hole. Or, it could involve trying to roll ball after ball so that each stops within a 3-foot radius. On the practice tee, repetition practice might be hitting shot after shot with the same club to the same target.

Repetition practice is an excellent way to groove a swing or shot. It is also a great way to learn to control your muscles and your swing so that the ball behaves the same way time and again. Repetition practice is an important way to practice and it applies to any type of shot, but it is boring, and it is not much like "real" golf. In golf, no two shots are alike.

Variation Practice

A critical aspect of ball control is for your child to be able to produce the correct shot, with the correct distance and aim when needed. Variation practice helps develop this skill by practicing shots that always differ in some way. An example of variation practice is putting to the same hole from different distances along the same line. Another example is using the same club on the range while hitting to a different target on each shot.

In the first example, your child will learn to adjust his stroke to account for the different distances, thereby controlling the speed of the ball. In the second example, your child will learn how to change his aim and focus on a new target with each swing.

Although variation practice is more like real golf than repetition practice, your child needs to use both methods. We all need to groove our swing so that it is repeatable and test it out in varying conditions.

Simulation Practice

Both repetition and variation practice are important, but they may not help improve the mental focus needed for your child to perform under pressure. Simulation practice, which involves simulating real playing conditions, can help. Essentially, this takes repetition or variation practice to the next level and simulates pressure situations. As an example, your child may practice repeated 3-foot putts. In simulation practice he would set a goal of sinking 50 of these 3-footers in a row. The more putts he sinks, the more pressure he will feel to succeed on the next try.

The pressure he will feel trying to make that 50th putt in a row is something like the pressure he feels on the course trying to make the same putt to win a tournament, or to shoot a personal best score. This approach also works for any type of shot, where each shot must succeed according to your child's standards.

Whether using repetition, variation, or simulation practice, I highly recommend keeping practice fun. Even if your child is more mature and beyond the stage where he needs games to make him practice, you may still find it helpful to make practice fun by using games to keep things interesting.

As an example, a great simulation game is "Sequence"[2], and it can be used with virtually any type of shot. Playing Sequence is simple: select a type of shot (e.g., a short putt, long putt, chip, pitch, bunker shot, or full swing with any club). Then define your target. For a short putt, it would be the hole. For a long putt or chip it might be a 3-foot radius around the hole. For a pitch or bunker shot it might be a 6-foot radius around the hole. For full shots it could be a green-sized target or a fairway-width area for drivers.

The object of Sequence is to hit as many shots in a row as possible that finish in your target. When practicing with a game like Sequence, your child should keep track of his performance and try to score a personal best each time he plays the game.

---

[2] Sequence is copyrighted by ParKit Golf, Inc. Used with permission.

Integration Practice

The final practice category is quite different, in that we are not so concerned with what the ball is doing. Rather, with integration practice, we are concerned with what the golfer is doing. This is where your child will practice swing mechanics or swing changes being made on the recommendation of his or her PGA/LPGA teaching professional.

Often, this type of practice is the most difficult, because it is so hard to ignore what the ball does. With integration practice, success

> *The ball changes everything*

can be defined by doing something the correct way, even if at first the ball refuses to behave.

For example, when I teach a student to make a grip change, I first want him to swing the club using the new grip, with no ball. I know it feels terrible, but I want him to get used to the feeling. Then, I want him to use the new grip while swinging at a ball. It is amazing how difficult this can be because when the ball is there, we all tend to revert back to old habits. Still, the crux of integration practice is for my student to use that new grip, that new swing, or that new stance while hitting a ball. If the ball doesn't immediately fly perfectly, no problem – as long as my student tries his best to use the new swing.

I know how hard it can be to get anyone, especially your child, to do something new and different about which they have little confidence. With my youngest students, I'll make it a challenge to see if they can do it to win "points" (every kid loves winning points... even if there is no point to the points). Or, I'll tell them that I know a secret of the pros and then balk at telling them until they beg to know it. "Only use this new grip if you want extra power," I'll say. "And don't tell anyone!" Before you know it his grip is stronger and the open clubface is a thing of the past.

The goal of integration practice is to adopt changes and incorporate them into your child's regular swing so that they become his "new normal" swing. These changes always require perseverance and patience to work through them while the ball may not be cooperating. Like learning other motor skills, the primary requirement is repetition… which can lead your child back to repetition practice as discussed above.

•   •   •

It is human nature to avoid boring, repetitive work and gravitate toward activities that are fun, exciting, and challenging. To that end, do everything in your power to keep practice fun and productive, and try not to force the process. If you can inject games into your child's practice sessions, he or she will practice for hours. And when practicing, make sure to include drills or games that cover each of the four categories of practice: repetition, variation, simulation, and integration.

If you need more specific ideas and tools to energize your child's practice sessions, check out the ParKit Short Game Kit at www.parkitgolf.com. ParKit's Short Game Kit is full of short game practice drills disguised as fun games that can really help improve your child's practice sessions and lower his scores (and yours, too). Another great tool for practice ideas is ParKit's "Encyclopedia of Fun Golf Games," which I wrote to bring all of our fun practice ideas together into a single book.

CHAPTER SEVEN

"The Great Pyramids of Egypt were built one block at a time."

The Golf Performance Pyramid

Even with hard work on game development, dedicated practice, and an outstanding coach and caddy (you), your child isn't guaranteed to achieve his or his peak level of golf performance. Indeed, peak performance is often determined by intangibles that are difficult to detect. Frequently, we "know it when we see it," but what is "it"? That elusive "it" factor is the wrapping that surrounds the whole package that is your child. It is where talent and coordination are combined with motivation, knowledge, focus, and self-confidence to produce a level of performance that is greater than the sum of its parts. It is where your child performs to his or her potential.

This does not mean that your child becomes a superstar. Rather, it means that your child becomes the best he can be; that he makes the most of his talents. But again, what is "it"?

I believe "it" can be described by what I call the "golf performance pyramid." This pyramid contains a foundation and building blocks that come together to show how to use one's talent and golf skills to reach peak levels of performance. Here is how I think the key building blocks of golf performance work… from the perspective of you, the parent.

The parental perspective is important here because your child may be too young to appreciate the importance of these building blocks. It may be up to you as his coach and caddy to supply the forethought and long-term view required to build his pyramid. Even if he is older and understands this process, your involvement is crucial, because you are there, on the bag, caddying, coordinating schedules, coaching and guiding him.

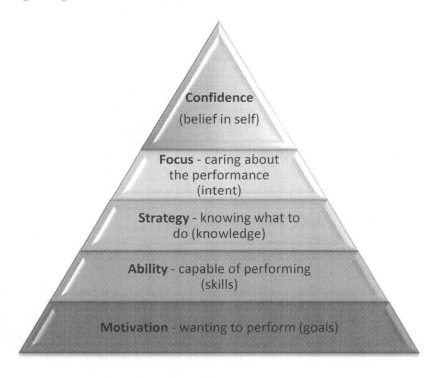

Figure 7.1: The Golf Performance Pyramid.

The building blocks of golf performance are motivation, ability, strategy, focus, and confidence. These five components differentiate ball-strikers from players, and good players from great players. If you want your child to perform to his potential, you need to help him incorporate these building blocks into his golf development.

Motivation

Performance begins with motivation, which is driven by inspiration, desire, dedication, and dreams... the inner drive to do what is necessary to learn and improve and achieve one's fullest potential. Motivation comes from goals that are lofty, yet reasonable and achievable. Without motivation, your child may have great golfing potential but it could be unrealized. As parents, one of our strongest desires is that our children will make the most of their talents and realize their potential, whether it be in golf or any other sport or activity.

Children are motivated to do what is fun and exciting, and that is the reason for my unending emphasis on having fun on and around the golf course. If it isn't fun, they won't want to do it, and their potential will remain just that: potential. They are also motivated to achieve personal goals... if those goals are *their own*. Your child may not be particularly motivated to achieve one of *your* goals.

Even later as their game improves and they mature, they must remain motivated to practice and improve. My experience has shown that a highly motivated but less talented player will almost always beat a more talented but less motivated player. Thus, motivation is the foundation of the performance pyramid, and it is the key to making the most of one's ability. Motivation brings your child to the golf course. It makes him want to putt for an hour. It makes him spend time on the range. And it makes him want to play golf and be the best he can be.

As his parent, you have a tremendous influence on your child's motivation. You can encourage, nurture, and support your child's interests. Or, you can pressure and push him and drive him away. You should help him identify his goals and objectives, and inspire him to work toward them. His resulting motivation will be his foundation to always try his best, to perform to the best of his abilities, and to strive to improve.

Ability

Next is ability – the combination of talent and skill that your child possesses that can be developed through self-discovery, practice, and instruction. Golf performance ultimately comes down to ball control, or the ability to make your golf ball go where you want it to go by controlling it's distance, direction, and trajectory with every club in the bag.

In your child's early golf development, swing mechanics and fundamentals may be secondary, as he just wants to enjoy hitting the ball over, under, or around things. I encourage my young students to develop these early ball control skills because they provide a sense of achievement and they motivate the student to do more.

Your young golfer's basic motor skills and coordination may not be strong, limiting his ability to perform. As he gets older and stronger, those skills will improve. In order to succeed later on, he will need to continue to refine his swing mechanics in order to continue to improve his ball control skills. If he has been motivated through having fun and achieving success, he will have the inner desire to learn and improve through instruction and productive practice.

In the performance pyramid, ability is a limiting factor – his level of ball control ability sets a limit on how low his scores can go. However, your child's ball control skills change over time through practice and experience. The rate and amount of this change is driven by the motivation building block discussed above.

Strategy

The third building block of golf performance is strategy. Strategy in this context refers to how your child uses his ball control abilities to play each hole. Strategy determines how he will play particular shots as they present themselves through a round of golf. In short, does he know what to do to make the most of his current skills? This means that his strategy will change over time in response to changes in his level of ability – the preceding building block in the pyramid.

In order to develop your child's strategy for a particular course, or as a general approach, you and he both need to have the necessary knowledge to know what to do. That includes:

— Self-knowledge of strengths and weaknesses. This requires an honest assessment of your child's ball control abilities and a true picture of what is possible. Can he carry that lake, or must he lay-up short? Should he risk hitting a driver into a tight fairway? Should he try to hit over or under that overhanging branch? The answers to these and many more questions are determined by his ball control skills.

— General knowledge of golf course design. Even if you are unfamiliar with a golf course, there are certain common design features that can influence your child's strategy. For example:

o Golf course architects love to create visual intimidation on the approach to greens. These features include yawning bunkers that must be carried, water hazards, and elevated greens. When it comes to club selection, don't count on your child hitting his perfect shot every time. It is better to use a club that does not have to be hit perfectly in der to reach the

> *Use a club that doesn't have to be hit perfectly to carry that bunker.*

target. We rarely hit perfect shots, so choose the "90%" club and allow for slight imperfections.

o It is better to leave the ball below the hole (leaving an uphill putt) than to be above the hole with a slippery, fast downhill putt.

o It is better to play wide on doglegs unless you are sure your child has the length to reach the middle of the fairway around the corner. Golf course architects like to entice us to cut the corner, only to find a hidden bunker or a strategically placed tree blocking our next shot.

o It may be better to hit into a bunker than into thick rough surrounding that same bunker.

o Junior golfers usually play age-appropriate yardages from tee markers that are in the fairway. This frequently means that their tee shots are landing in difficult areas around greens and where fairways narrow. These golf course design features were intended to catch stray approach shots – not tee shots. It could be wise to use less than a driver on some holes in order to leave an easier approach shot to the green.

While the above examples are fairly basic, there are many features of golf course design that can influence playing strategy. There is no shortcut to learning these other than playing lots of golf and paying attention to course layouts and design features. The more familiar you and your child are with these factors, the better his strategy will become.

— Specific course knowledge. In many cases, there is no substitute for being familiar with the course being played. When I help prep a student in a practice round, we develop a comprehensive plan for how to play each hole based on his skills and abilities. This plan represents the best strategy for producing his lowest score, and is aggressive where possible and defensive where necessary.

Ultimately, to achieve his best performance, your child needs to make good decisions and play to his strengths. Your job as caddy is to bring a clear-headed, mature mind to the scene and provide strategic advice. The best approach is always to discuss these strategic decisions ahead of time, before the heat of the battle and competitive pressures can combine to force a last-second change or cause indecision over the ball.

Focus

So your child is motivated and inspired to practice and improve his ball control skills, and he has a strategic plan of attack for the course. Then, prior to hitting his next shot, he is distracted by a jumbo jet flying low overhead, or a motorcycle speeding on a nearby highway, or a big tractor trailer nearby, or a butterfly, or suddenly being hungry, or goofing around and taking funny practice swings, or... you know what I am talking about. This loss of focus is guaranteed to produce a poor shot, where his skills are compromised and his strategy is forgotten.

It is very difficult for anyone, much less a child, to focus and concentrate on something for as long as it takes to play nine holes of competitive golf (figure three to four hours, including warm-up time). Therefore, it is important to allow your child to, well, act like a child at times, and be playful occasionally between shots. There is a fine line between being playful and losing control, so you need to be the judge of your own child's tendencies. And, you need to be respectful of other players (and their daddy caddies) who may not appreciate this approach.

My point here is to allow your child to relax and enjoy the experience of being with friends and fellow competitors. Even PGA Tour professionals relax, joke around, and get their minds off the game between shots. In Steve Williams' book "Golf at the Top," he relates how one of his most important functions was to talk to Tiger about anything *but* golf between shots. Golf is intense; relaxation is imperative. What is important then is to be able to re-focus when it is time to perform.

In the chapter on managing the mental game I discussed the importance of a pre-shot routine, and that is the key to regaining focus before hitting the shot. A pre-shot routine can help your child develop the ability to alternately focus and relax; to get into the game at shot time, and to have fun in between.

Focusing on the shot requires concentration and a commitment to the strategic plan, and most importantly, caring about the outcome of the shot. It requires the *intent* to do his best on the shot. It requires the belief that nothing else matters – neither the 3-putt on the last green nor the beautiful trophy waiting for him – only this next shot.

Confidence

The peak of the peak golf performance pyramid is confidence. None of the other steps matter if your child does not have the confidence that he can perform. He must believe that he has the ability to hit the shot and that his strategy for the shot is the best for him. In a sense, confidence, or lack thereof, is another kind of distraction or loss of focus. However, confidence is so much more, and it pervades your child's very demeanor and approach to golf.

Confidence is a serious challenge with the game of golf, because it is so easy to make a mistake or to mis-hit a shot. Fortunately, we all hit good shots, at least occasionally! These good shots can provide good memories and instill confidence for future shots.

As his caddy, your job is to remember those good shots and help your child conjure up those memories as he prepares to swing. I can remember at least one good shot my son has hit with every club, and I'll remind him of it each time. Golf is such a mental game that simply picturing that good shot can free up the golf swing as we try to re-create it each time. It doesn't always work, but no one has ever hit a good shot when he lacked the confidence that he could do it.

●   ●   ●

Great scores happen when all of the elements of the golf performance pyramid come together. Your child was motivated to practice for the tournament. His ball control abilities are the best they can be – for him, right now. He has a solid strategy for scoring. He can focus on each shot. And he has the self-confidence that he can perform. This winning combination can produce his best performance, whether it is to win the tournament or to shoot a personal best score. Both are victories that should be celebrated!

CHAPTER EIGHT

"So often our own children teach us the lessons we need to learn."

– MARGO COHEN

The 19th Hole

The threatening weather remained just far enough away for us to finish our practice round without delays. And what an amazing round it was. Alex and I were both relaxed, and we joined up with another father-son pair who were also enjoying themselves. The other boy was in a different age group, so Alex felt no pressure to compare their games.

His swing was relaxed and powerful. Approach shots flew true. Putts fell into holes that seemed larger than usual. We laughed and high-fived our way around, and the round was over before we knew it. It seemed almost impossible that he had shot a 6-under par score of 30. The golf was fun; even easy. Tension was non-existent. The daddy caddy – player relationship was true teamwork, and his potential was revealed.

If I have any overarching ambition, it is to enable every junior golfer to see a glimpse of their own potential the way Alex saw his that day. I believe the road to our children's potential lies beneath the emotional noise and interference that we all introduce without even realizing it. And, I believe that if we can simplify our conflicting roles as parents, coaches, and caddies and stay out of their way, our children will find the road for themselves. When they do, their discovery will be much more valuable to them than it would be coming from us.

I have always enjoyed using other sports as examples for teaching golf. In this case, I think the Olympic sport of curling is the perfect metaphor for coaching your child. If you are not familiar with it, curling shares some similarities with shuffleboard or lawn bowling, but with a twist. Curling is a winter sport that is played on ice, and it is that twist that makes curling so interesting. A curler gives a large smooth stone a push toward a goal. Once the stone is sliding on the ice, two teammates with brooms (they are called sweepers) rush ahead of the stone and influence its movement by sweeping the ice and snow in front of the moving stone. The sweepers cannot touch the stone, but they can change its speed or direction and help it reach the goal by sweeping ice to one side or the other.

As golf parents, coaches, mentors, and caddies for our children, I think we should do the same. We give our children a push in the right direction to get them moving, and then we should stay ahead and clear their path so that it leads to their goal. When they wander, we should guide them back on track by leading and showing them the way. It is when we stay behind them, continuing to push or steer that our task becomes difficult and their resistance grows.

Ultimately, the objective of this book is to help us daddy caddies become better curlers and sweepers. If you are going to caddy for your child, be a great caddy and give your child a motivational push in the right direction. Then, be a leader and guide him through his round by following your caddy job description while you are on the bag. Great caddies are teammates, but they know their player is the boss. Great caddies are supportive, knowledgeable, encouraging, and give their player great advice... and let their player make his own decisions. If you are not a golfer, consider becoming one so that you will better appreciate what your child is going through.

As your child's caddy, you are with him in the action, and you can help him manage his emotions. As painful as it might be, great caddies absorb the emotional heat and keep their player on a positive and even keel. Great caddies sweep away doubt, anger, and fear and allow their player to shine.

If you are also your child's golf coach, be a great coach. Whether you follow the coaching program described herein or develop your own approach, ensure that your coaching system addresses all aspects of your child's game. Help motivate your child by keeping the process fun and start him on the path to his goals. Then, guide and mentor him and show him how to reach those goals from a position of leadership. Great coaches sweep away obstacles and allow their student to succeed.

Finally, keep things in perspective. Your child is still young, and he or she is playing this amazing lifelong game. There will be triumphs and setbacks aplenty, because that is the nature of golf.

However difficult it is for us to caddy for or coach our own children, playing golf is even harder. Along the way, they are learning and growing and maturing into golfers. As they do, they are also teaching us the lessons we need to learn in order to help them flourish. I can only hope that we are great students!

Appendix 1

Skills Assessment Worksheets

The first step on the road to improvement is to find out where you are right now. But how do you know where you are and where your improvement opportunities lie? To paraphrase the great physicist Lord Kelvin, "you can't improve what you can't measure," and it is true. You need a way to measure your current skill level so that you can determine which skills need the most improvement. And, in order to measure your skills, you need information. That information comes from a skills evaluation.

The following skills assessment worksheets can help assess your strengths and improvement opportunities across all areas of your game. These worksheets provide detailed data that can be used to develop a comprehensive improvement plan for those who want to make a significant improvement in their scores.

Done properly, a skills evaluation will provide a measurement of the status of your game at a point in time. A proper evaluation will provide information that can be used to identify those high priority areas that have the greatest impact on lowering your scores. Repeated evaluations taken over time will show trends in your skills – hopefully becoming better and better!

There are two ways to evaluate your skills:

1. Conduct periodic skills evaluations using a standard skills assessment format, and

2. Record your performance statistics during tournament or serious rounds of golf where you play by USGA rules (see Appendix 2).

The Skills Assessment Worksheets may be used to collect skills assessment data in the following scoring areas:

— Short putts from 3 to 15 feet

— Long putts from 20 to 60 feet

— Chipping from 45 feet and 60 feet

— Pitching from 25 to 30 yards from the hole

— Bunkers from 10-15 yards from the hole

— Approach shots from 20, 40, 60, 80, and 100 yards

— Carry distances with wedge, 6-iron, and 3-wood

— Ball control ability to produce nine different ball flights

Your child should make a habit of doing each evaluation at regular intervals – perhaps monthly or every two months. Record the date of each evaluation and monitor progress over time.

The following pages contain detailed instructions for setting up each skills assessment and for using the worksheets. As part of your child's golf development program, you should periodically conduct a skills contest where your child does the skills assessments shown on the worksheets.

Short Putt

Find a location on the putting green where you can putt from 3 feet to 15 feet from the hole with a slight break from left to right. Measure points at 3-foot intervals, beginning at 3 feet from the hole. Place a ball marker on each spot. When complete, you should have markers at 3', 6', 9', 12', and 15'. All putts should be along the same line, with a slight left to right break.

Begin at the 3' mark and attempt two putts. If you sink a putt, record a "0" on the worksheet. If the putt misses, record the distance in feet of each miss, always rounding up to the next number of feet. For example, any miss is "1." If you miss by 1½ feet, write down "2", and so on. Note whether your misses are due to distance control or aiming issues. Do this from each of the markers, then repeat from a different spot on the green with a slight right to left break.

Total your results from each side of the worksheet and compare to your prior values. You should look for trends and differences in the results. Are you better with putts that break right or left? Is there a length of putt that is problematic? Is distance control a problem? Are you showing improvement from prior assessments?

DLGA Skills Assessment Worksheet: Short Putt

Date	Breaking Left to Right										L-R TOTAL	Breaking Right to Left										R-L TOTAL	TOTAL ALL
	3'		6'		9'		12'		15'			3'		6'		9'		12'		15'			
	1	2	1	2	1	2	1	2	1	2		1	2	1	2	1	2	1	2	1	2		

20 putts in all. Take 2 putts from each distance. Record the resulting distance in feet from the hole for each putt. Record "0" if the ball finishes in the hole.

Long Putt

Find a place on the putting green where you can putt from 20 feet to 60 feet from the hole. Measure points at 20', 30', 40', 50', and 60' and place a ball marker on each spot. All putts should be along the same line.

Begin at the 20' mark and attempt two putts. If you sink a putt, record a "0" on the worksheet. If the putt misses, record the distance in feet of each miss, always rounding up to the next number of feet. For example, any miss is "1." If you miss by 1½ feet, write down "2", and so on. Do this from each of the markers, then total your results for all putts combined.

Total your results across each length of putt and compare to your prior values. You should look for trends and differences in the results. Long putts require excellent distance control. Is there a length of putt that is problematic? Are you showing improvement from prior assessments?

DLGA Skills Assessment Worksheet   Long Putt

Date	20'		30'		40'		50'		60'		TOTAL ALL
	1	2	1	2	1	2	1	2	1	2	

10 putts in all, to same hole from different distances. Take 2 putts from each distance. Record the resulting distance in feet from the hole for each putt. Record "0" if the ball finishes in the hole.

Chipping

Find a place on fringe of the putting green where you will have a good lie and can chip from 45 feet and 60 feet to different holes. All chips should be across a flat green with little or no break.

Begin at the 45' mark and attempt five chips. If you sink the chip, record a "0" on the worksheet. If the chip misses, record the distance in feet of each miss, always rounding up to the next number of feet. For example, any miss is "1." If you miss by 1½ feet, write down "2", and so on. If you miss by more than 20 feet, record "21." Do this from each distance and total your results for each distance.

Total your results from each side of the worksheet and compare to your prior values. You should look for trends and differences in the results. Is there a length of chip that is problematic? Are you showing improvement from prior assessments?

DLGA Skills Assessment Worksheet: Chipping

Date	From 45 Feet					45' TOTAL	From 60 Feet					60' TOTAL	TOTAL ALL
	1	2	3	4	5		1	2	3	4	5		

10 shots in all, from the fringe. Take 5 shots from each distance. Measure and record the resulting distance in feet from the hole for each chip. Record "0" if the ball finishes in the hole. Record "21" if the ball finishes more than 20 feet from the hole.

Pitching

Find a place 15 yards from the edge of the putting green where you will have a good lie and can pitch approximately 25-30 yards from the hole. There should be around 10-15 yards from the edge of the green to the hole, in addition to the 15 yards from the pitching location to the edge of the green. Select a location where the ball can land and roll across a flat green with little or no break.

Attempt ten pitch shots. If you sink the shot, record a "0" on the worksheet. If the shot misses, record the distance in feet of each miss, always rounding up to the next number of feet. For example, any miss is "1." If you miss by 1½ feet, write down "2", and so on. If you miss by more than 20 feet, record "21." Total your results for all shots combined.

Total your results for all 10 shots and compare to your prior values. You should look for trends and differences in the results. How consistent are you? Do your shots tend to come up short or go too long? Do you tend to hit pitch shots "thin" (not brushing the grass) or "fat" (hitting grass behind the ball)? Are you showing improvement from prior assessments?

DLGA Skills Assessment Worksheet: Pitching

Date	1	2	3	4	5	6	7	8	9	10	TOTAL

10 shots in all, from a good lie 20-25 yards from the green. Measure and record the resulting distance in feet from the hole for each shot. Record "0" if the ball finishes in the hole. Record "21" if the ball finishes more than 20 feet from the hole.

Bunkers

Find a place in a greenside bunker where you will have a good lie about 10-15 yards from the hole. The shot should be across a flat green with little or no break.

Attempt ten bunker shots. Rake the bunker as necessary between shots so that each shot is from a nice flat lie If you sink the shot, record a "0" on the worksheet. If the shot misses, record the distance in feet of each miss, always rounding up to the next number of feet. For example, any miss is "1." If you miss by 1½ feet, write down "2", and so on. If you miss by more than 20 feet, record "21." Total your results for all shots combined.

Total your results for all 10 shots and compare to your prior values. You should look for trends and differences in the results. How consistent are you? Do your shots tend to come up short or go too long? Do you tend to hit bunker shots "thin" (not taking enough sand) or "fat" (hitting too much sand or too far behind the ball)? Are you showing improvement from prior assessments?

DLGA Skills Assessment Worksheet: Bunkers

Date	1	2	3	4	5	6	7	8	9	10	TOTAL

10 shots in all, from a good lie in a greenside bunker. Measure and record the resulting distance in feet from the hole for each shot. Record "0" if the ball finishes in the hole. Record "21" if the ball finishes more than 20 feet from the hole.

Approach Shots

Find a place in a fairway where you can hit approach shots to a green. If this is not possible, you may use the driving range if you will be able to measure how far away your shots will come to rest from a target. Use a laser range finder and measure points at 20, 40, 60, 80, and 100 yards from the hole or your range target. It is best to do this assessment with a partner who can measure and record each shot after you hit it.

Begin at the 20 yard mark and attempt two shots. Record the distance in feet that each ball comes to rest from the hole or target, always rounding up to the next number of feet. For example, if the ball finishes 1½ feet from the hole, write down "2", and so on. If your ball finishes more than 40 feet from the hole, record "41." Do the same from each yardage.

Total your results for all 10 shots and compare to your prior values. You should look for trends and differences in the results. How consistent are you? Is there a distance that is more difficult for you? Are you changing clubs as the distances change, or do you use the same club for each shot? Do your shots tend to come up short or go too long? Is there a pattern of missing to the right or to the left? Are you showing improvement from prior assessments?

DLGA Skills Assessment Worksheet: Approach Shots

Date	20 Yards		40 Yards		60 Yards		80 Yards		100 Yards		TOTAL ALL
	1	2	1	2	1	2	1	2	1	2	

10 shots in all. Take 2 shots from each distance. Record the resulting distance in feet from the hole for each shot. Record "0" if the shot finishes in the hole. Record "41" if the ball finishes more than 40 feet from the hole.

Carry Distances

Every golfer needs to know the exact yardage the ball carries with each club. This worksheet provides a way for you to record your carry distances with your pitching wedge, 6-iron and 3-wood. Your distances with other clubs probably increase in 7-10 yard increments, but you can also measure them individually and record them on another worksheet.

Using each club from a good lie in the fairway or on the driving range, hit five balls. Watch where each shot lands and measure the distance with a laser range finder. It is best to do this assessment with a partner who can measure and record each shot after you hit it. Record the yardage on the worksheet.

Pay close attention to your results, especially to variations in carry distance. You want to be able to hit each club with consistent, predictable carry yardages to help you make the proper club selection on the course. If you have wide variations due to poor shots, exclude those from the averages and use only the more consistent shots. Then, think about those poor shots and their causes. Use face impact tape to determine whether you are consistently hitting the ball on the "sweet spot." Do you tend to hit these shots "thin" (not brushing the grass) or "fat" (hitting the grass behind the ball)?

Daddy Caddy On the Bag   Carry Distance Skills Assessment Worksheet

Date	Wedge					6-Iron					3-Wood				
	1	2	3	4	5	1	2	3	4	5	1	2	3	4	5

15 shots in all. Hit 5 shots with a full swing with each club. Measure and record the actual total distance the ball travels in the air (use a laser measuring device, or place cones or other markers on the range at known distances).

Nine Ball Flights

This worksheet helps you measure your ability to control your golf ball. Golf seldom demands perfectly straight shots, and you need to be able to work the ball, making it curve and controlling its trajectory at will. This skill is especially important in poor weather conditions and for trouble shots, where you might need to hit shots low or high, or curve the ball around obstacles.

Do this assessment at the range, and work through the nine ball flights. Try to make the ball hook, go straight, and slice on command. Try to hit low, medium, and high shots. Record a "1" on the worksheet if you are successful at a particular shot, and total your score to see if you can score 9 points.

You should incorporate the Nine Ball Flights into every practice session... it is fun to practice controlling your ball flight. And, learning to hook and slice the ball at will can be the best way to learn to hit the ball straight.

Daddy Caddy On the Bag   Nine Ball Flights Worksheet

Date	Low Hook	Medium Hook	High Hook	Low Straight	Medium Straight	High Straight	Low Slice	Medium Slice	High Slice	TOTAL

The purpose is to learn to control the ball flight. Make 1 attempt at each shot, trying to hit the type of shot described in each column. Make a check mark if the shot is successful.

Appendix 2

Golf Statistics Scorecard

The second and perhaps best way to evaluate your skill level is through your performance during actual rounds of golf where you play by USGA rules. If your child is already playing tournament golf, these are perfect opportunities to learn more about his or her performance. If not, they can still play rounds and record their statistics.

The following "stats scorecard" provides a way to record some of the most important performance statistics as your child plays. Bring this scorecard with you and enter his or her results at the end of each hole, as you would normally write down their score.

A common mistake in collecting performance data is to try to capture too much information. Sometimes, all that is really needed is stats on greens hit in regulation scrambling, and putting. However, if you really want to understand the factors that are driving your child's scores, you should record all of his or her results from this scorecard.

In order to capture the information quickly, it is important to keep the process simple. If you use the following method, you will be able to maintain useful performance statistics on each round of golf. Here are suggestions for each entry line:

Golf Statistics Scorecard Instructions

Par – Enter the hole-by-hole par for the course you are playing.

Hit Fairway – Enter a code for the club used from the tee on par 4 and par 5 holes (e.g. "D" for driver). Circle or otherwise mark the box if the shot finds the fairway.

Green in Regulation – Enter the club used for the approach to the green. Circle or otherwise mark the box if the shot finds the green.

Scramble Attempt – Enter the club used for a chip or pitch from around the green. Circle or otherwise mark the box if you successfully scramble (get on the green and 1-putt).

Greenside Bunker – Enter the club used for a bunker shot. Circle or otherwise mark the box if you get on the green and 1-putt.

Penalties – Enter a code as shown on the card for any penalties you may incur, such as out of bounds, water hazard, lost ball, etc.

 # Putts – Enter the number of putts, counting only shots taken from the green. If the ball is off the green it is a scramble attempt.

Score – Record your score for the hole.

When you are finished recording your child's information for a round, take time to look over the stats and understand what he or she did well and what areas need improvement

Daddy Caddy On the Bag   Golf Stats Scorecard   Date: Course:

Hole	1	2	3	4	5	6	7	8	9	TOTAL
Par										
Hit Fairway										
Green in Regulation										
Scramble Attempt										
Greenside Bunker										
Penalties										
# Putts										
Score										

Green in Regulation means on the green in 1 shot on par 3, 2 shots on par 4, and 3 shots on par 5 holes. Scramble Attempt means shots taken (with any club) within 15 yards of the green.

Penalties coded as follows:

OB	out of bounds	W	water hazard
U	unplayable lie	L	lost ball
B	ball moved	O	other